Series / Number 07-054

MULTIVARIATE ANALYSIS OF VARIANCE

JAMES H. BRAY
Texas Woman's University
Houston Center

SCOTT E. MAXWELL
University of Notre Dame

SAGE PUBLICATIONS
The International Professional Publishers
Newbury Park   London   New Delhi

For information address:

 SAGE Publications, Inc.
2455 Teller Road
Newbury Park, California 91320
E-mail: order@sagepub.com

SAGE Publications Ltd.
6 Bonhill Street
London EC2A 4PU
United Kingdom

SAGE Publications India Pvt. Ltd.
M-32 Market
Greater Kailash I
New Delhi 110 048 India

Printed in the United States of America

International Standard Book Number 0-8039-2310-4

Library of Congress Catalog Card No. L.C. 85-062142

99   00   01   02   18   17   16   15   14

When citing a University Paper, please use the proper form. Remember to cite the correct Sage University Paper series title and include the paper number. One of the following formats can be adapted (depending on the style manual used):

(1) BRAY, JAMES H. and SCOTT E. MAXWELL (1985) *Multivariate Analysis of Variance*. Sage University Paper Series on Quantitative Research Methods, Vol. 54. Newbury Park, CA: Sage.

or

(2) Bray, J. H. & Maxwell, S. E. (1985). *Multivariate analysis of variance* (Sage University Paper Series on Qualitative Research Methods, Vol. 54). Newbury Park, CA: Sage.

CONTENTS

Series Editor's Introduction

Analysis of variance (ANOVA) is one of the most frequently employed statistical techniques in the social sciences, particularly in the fields of Psychology, Educational Psychology, and Sociology, because it provides a flexible methodology for testing differences among means. This monograph on *Multivariate Analysis of Variance* builds on Iversen and Norpoth's *Analysis of Variance,* published earlier in this series. Readers should be familiar with the material presented by Iversen and Norpoth before undertaking this monograph.

Multivariate analysis of variance (MANOVA) is a generalization of analysis of variance that allows the researcher to analyze more than one dependent variable. Many times it is of interest to compare group means on several variables simultaneously, and MANOVA allows the researcher to do this in both experimental and observational research. Bray and Maxwell show the reader how ANOVA is generalized to MANOVA and provide examples to illustrate its proper use.

The primary emphasis in this presentation is on interpreting the results from MANOVA analyses. There are two numerical examples that appear throughout the text, one involving a small, hypothetical data set and the other involving actual data and showing how MANOVA is used in actual research. As such, this manuscript provides a unique perspective and a treatment that nicely complements most textbook treatments of the topic. Chapter 2 contains discussions of such issues as the assumptions underlying the technique, their robustness, statistical power of MANOVA, and various measures of strength of association. Chapter 3 presents the variety of methods available for interpreting the meaning of an omnibus significant test result. As in univariate ANOVA, it is commonly necessary to conduct a follow-up analysis to determine the precise nature of the differences among means implied by an omnibus test. Chapter 4 considers MANOVA and its follow-up test with a use of path diagrams, to further develop the reader's conceptual understanding of the differences and similarities among the various tests. Chapter 5 is a brief introduction to complex

5

designs, and Chapter 6 presents an overview of the computer software available for performing MANOVA.

Bray and Maxwell have provided us with a readable and excellent introduction to MANOVA. As the social sciences slowly mature, researchers are realizing more and more that our statistical techniques must be capable of testing increasingly complex theoretical and conceptual ideas and of estimating models that incorporate more and more of this complexity. Simple ANOVA models have their uses, of course, but the simultaneous analysis of multiple dependent variables is one step toward understanding and analyzing the complexity we all know exists in the "real world."

—John L. Sullivan
Series Co-Editor

MULTIVARIATE ANALYSIS OF VARIANCE

JAMES H. BRAY
Texas Woman's University
Houston Center

SCOTT E. MAXWELL
University of Notre Dame

1. INTRODUCTION TO MULTIVARIATE ANALYSIS OF VARIANCE

The application of multivariate analysis of variance (MANOVA) in the behavioral sciences has increased dramatically, and it appears that it will be used frequently in the future for data analysis. Although the mathematical basis of MANOVA and related techniques was largely developed in the 1930s and 1940s, only in recent years have the techniques been applied in the social sciences. This increase is largely due to the availability of accessible computer programs that simplify the tedious calculations required. The result is the application of these sophisticated techniques to a wide variety of research problems.

MANOVA is a conceptually straightforward extension of the well-known univariate ANOVA techniques. The major distinction is that in ANOVA one evaluates mean differences on a single dependent criterion variable, whereas in MANOVA one evaluates mean differences on two

AUTHORS' NOTE: *The two authors contributed equally to the preparation of the work. Dr. Bray's contribution was supported by grant 1 ROI HD18025-01 from the National Institute of Child Health and Human Development of the National Institutes of Health. Sections 3 and 4 of this work are a modified draft of J. H. Bray and S. E. Maxwell, "Analyzing and interpreting significant MANOVAs,"* Review of Education Research 52 *(1982): 340-367. Copyright by the American Educational Research Association. This material is reprinted with permission of the AERA.*

7

or more dependent criterion variables simultaneously. Although ANOVA and MANOVA are often associated with experimental studies involving a manipulation introduced by the experimenter, both techniques are in fact appropriate whenever the research question involves a comparison of mean scores. For example, the average (i.e., mean) scores for females and males might be compared on a battery of intellectual measures, or the average political attitudes of city dwellers might be compared to those of people in rural areas. When means on single variables are to be compared, ANOVA is appropriate (if its assumptions are reasonably satisfied). However, when means on several different variables are to be compared simultaneously, MANOVA is usually necessary (again, contingent on meeting a set of assumptions to be discussed later).

Like ANOVA, MANOVA is usually conducted as a two-step process. The first step is to test the overall hypothesis of no differences in the means for the different groups (i.e., the overall or omnibus test). If this test is significant, the second step is to conduct follow-up tests to explain group differences. The mathematical basis for applying MANOVA is well known and generally accepted (see Bock, 1975; Finn, 1974; Timm, 1975). However, two broad areas are still in development: (1) issues concerning the overall test, such as choice between test statistics, power and sample size concerns, and measures of effect size, and (2) methods for further analyzing and interpreting group differences when an overall significant MANOVA is found. There is currently considerable controversy on these topics, with little consensus as to the "proper" use of the methods (Borgen and Seling, 1978; Bray and Maxwell, 1982; Gabriel, 1979; Kaplan and Litownik, 1977; Larrabbe, 1982; Leary and Altmaier, 1980; O'Grady, 1978; Spector, 1977, 1980; Stevens, 1972; Strahan, 1982; Wilkinson, 1975). In addition, there is a more recent trend to understand MANOVA and related techniques in the context of the General Linear Model and their relationship to structural models that underlie the methods (Bray and Maxwell, 1982; Kenny, 1979).

The purpose of this book is to comprehensively review and discuss the use of MANOVA and related techniques in the behavioral sciences. The book will focus on three areas: (1) developing a conceptual understanding of MANOVA, appropriate application, and issues in the use of the MANOVA method; (2) procedures for analyzing and interpreting significant MANOVAs; and (3) the causal models underlying MANOVA and their relationship to other multivariate techniques. The position we take is that there is no one "right" method but, instead, that there are advantages and disadvantages to each, which depend on what the researcher hopes to glean from the data. The approach taken will be nonmathematical and will focus on the appropriate use and interpretation of the various methods. In this regard, we will provide some decision rules to facilitate researchers choosing the appropriate techniques for their study.

Use of Multiple Criterion Variables

A reasonable question to ask is why use more than one criterion variable? In most cases researchers are not interested in a single measure of group differences. Rather, there are usually several components, constructs, or behaviors that might be affected by the treatment or that are useful to separate the groups.

For example, if we wanted to evaluate the effects of a training program to increase assertiveness, we might be interested in measuring the effects of the training program on the person's (1) assertive behavior, (2) anxiety about being assertive, and (3) self-esteem. It might reasonably be expected that there would be a non-zero correlation between these variables because they measure different aspects of assertion. In this case MANOVA provides a distinct advantage over separate ANOVAs because the MANOVA test considers the correlations between the variables. In fact, if separate ANOVA tests are performed it is implicitly assumed that either the correlations between the variables are zero or that the correlations are not of interest (more on this in Section 3). In addition, even if the major interest is in assessing the effects on only one construct, it is almost always the case that it is better to multi-operationalize a construct (i.e., have several measures of it), rather than mono-operationalize the construct (i.e., have a single measure of it; Cook and Campbell, 1979). Particularly in the social sciences, in which measurement is considerably less than perfect, multi-operationalizing constructs and using multivariate methods to assess the effects of treatments may provide a more valid assessment of treatment effects (Cole et al., 1981).

A note of caution is warranted here. First, the indiscriminant use of multiple dependent measures is never an appropriate substitute for a well-conceived study with a select number of variables. Just conducting a study and measuring everything related to one's area of interest is a poor substitute for a more controlled design in which a small number of reliable measures are employed. Although MANOVA allows the researcher to handle multiple dependent variables, these should be selected carefully to accurately measure the effects of interest. In fact, the use of too many dependent variables may hinder the chances of finding a significant result because of low statistical power or it may result in spurious findings due to chance. These last two issues will be discussed further in Sections 2 and 3.

Relationship of ANOVA to MANOVA

In an ANOVA we test the null hypothesis that the means of k groups (where k = the number of groups) are all equal to one another. In this case we are testing whether there are significant differences between the groups on a single dependent variable.

In the multivariate case we test the null hypothesis that the population means of the k groups are equal to one another for all p variables. This is a test that the k group centroids are equal. (A centroid is the p-dimensional vector of population means for that group.) With one MANOVA approach we are testing whether there are significant differences between groups on a new variate, called a centroid, that maximally separates the groups. (A *variable* refers to one of the criteria that is observed and measured in the study, whereas a *variate* is a statistical criterion resulting from a linear combination of the original observed variables.) In one sense an ANOVA is performed on the new criterion variate, the weighted linear combination of the p variables. (It is important to note that the above statement is limited to one MANOVA approach.) Unlike the univariate case, there is not just one method (i.e., the F test) to form a test statistic. Instead, there are several methods. A more complete discussion and comparison of these methods will be developed and presented in Section 2.

Why Use MANOVA?

There are several reasons to use MANOVA in studies investigating mean differences. First, researchers are typically interested in evaluating mean differences on several criterion variables, rather than a single criterion variable. Even if the researcher is only interested in these differences on each variable individually, MANOVA may still be the optimal technique. In this case, MANOVA is used to control the overall alpha level at the desired level (usually .05), but the researcher is interested only in the separate univariate analyses that may subsequently be performed. Another alternative in this situation, which will be discussed later, is to perform separate ANOVAs with a Bonferroni adjustment of the alpha level (Bird, 1975; Timm, 1975).

A second major reason to use MANOVA is because the researcher wants to look at the relationships among the variables rather than looking at each of them in isolation. That is, the researcher wants to evaluate the mean differences on all of the dependent variables simultaneously, while controlling for the intercorrelations among them. In this case there are several potential uses to consider: (1) the researcher wants to look at the relationships among the p variables for the group comparisons; (2) the researcher wishes to reduce the p variables to some smaller set of theoretical dimensions; (3) the researcher wants to select the variables that contribute most to group separation; and/or (4) the researcher is interested in the *set* of measures as they represent some underlying construct(s). In each of these cases there is the opportunity to learn more about the data by looking at the variables in some combination or pattern rather than individually. This is where MANOVA offers some unique advantages over separate ANOVAs.

To further exemplify the differences between ANOVA and MANOVA, consider the case in which we have an experiment with two groups of teachers: Group 1 subjects receive a treatment to improve their teaching and Group 2 subjects serve as controls. In this case we are interested in whether the treatment improves teaching as measured by two criterion variables: student ratings and peer ratings of teaching quality. Hypothetical data for this example are illustrated in Figure 1.1. The axes represent the frequency distributions for each variable. If we look at each variable individually, it appears that the distributions overlap sufficiently that it is unlikely that we would find significant effects on either of the ANOVAs separately. However, the MANOVA looks at the two-dimensional space simultaneously. Figure 1.2 illustrates a possible bivariate frequency distribution for the two-dimensional space. Here we notice that the groups are more separated in the two-dimensional space than in either dimension individually.

Thus, one benefit of MANOVA is that by examining both variables together, it may provide a more powerful test than doing separate ANOVAs.

Another potential benefit of MANOVA is that interpretation of results may be enhanced by considering criterion variables simultaneously. As mentioned above, one way of conceptualizing MANOVA is that it forms a new criterion for each subject, which is that linear combination of the p variables that maximally separates the groups. In other words, when $p = 2$ (for simplicity), MANOVA finds a criterion of the form:

$$V_{ij} = k_1 Y_1 + k_2 Y_2$$

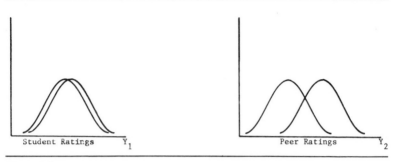

Figure 1.1

where k_1 is the weight for variable Y_1 and k_2 is the weight for variable Y_2. This new criterion has the property that mean differences are maximized relative to within-group variance on this variable. Any other linear combination of Y_1 and Y_2 would produce more overlap between the distributions. Because the linear combination found by MANOVA maximizes group differences, it is often informative to interpret MANOVA results based on the magnitude of the weights derived for each of the dependent variables (see further discussion in Sections 2 and 3).

Although MANOVA may sometimes provide a more useful and valid means of analyzing data, this is not always the case. There are some situations in which MANOVA is unnecessary. If a researcher plans to only use dependent variables that are uncorrelated, there is little advantage for using MANOVA. In fact, with uncorrelated criteria and relatively small sample size, MANOVA may be at a disadvantage to separate ANOVAs in terms of statistical power. Second, the results from an analysis using MANOVA may be more complex and difficult to interpret than those from ANOVAs. Although this complexity may accurately reflect the phenomena under study, multivariate statistics can be more difficult to understand and consequently make the interpretation more complex. The reverse situation can also be true; that is, MANOVA may sometimes simplify the data and make them more understandable. Thus, the researcher is wise to seriously consider both the advantages and the disadvantages before using MANOVA or any statistical technique *before* collecting the data.

In the following sections we will discuss the overall or omnibus MANOVA test, issues concerning the selection of the appropriate test statistic, and related considerations, such as power and measures of effect size. Section 3 will present the various methods for analyzing and interpreting a significant MANOVA, and Section 4 will describe the

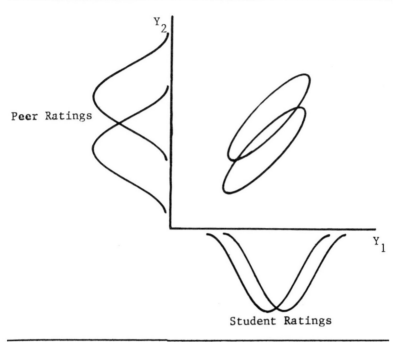

Figure 1.2

causal models underlying MANOVA analyses. Section 5 will briefly discuss the use of MANOVA in more complex designs. The last section will review the popular statistical computer packages for MANOVA.

2. OMNIBUS MANOVA TESTS

The omnibus or overall MANOVA test is the first step in the MA-NOVA procedure. It is analogous to the overall F test in ANOVA. In the univariate case this F test is the uniformly most powerful invariant test of the overall null hypothesis if its assumptions are met. However, in MANOVA there is no single invariant test that is uniformly most powerful, even if all assumptions have been satisfied. For this reason, in MANOVA there are several test statistics that might be used to evaluate the overall null hypothesis. Because the various test statistics are based on different mathematical criteria, the results of a study may differ depending on the test statistic chosen. In this chapter the various MANOVA test statistics will be discussed. In addition, issues related to the overall MANOVA test will be presented. Before discussing the various MANOVA test criteria, it is important to understand the multivariate null hypothesis.

Multivariate Null Hypothesis

Before considering hypothesis testing in MANOVA, we will briefly review the univariate case. For the sake of simplicity, we will only deal with a single factor design: that is, a situation in which there is no factorial structure imposed on the groupings of subjects. However, the relationships between the univariate and multivariate approaches we will develop in this special case also hold for more complex designs. In ANOVA the purpose is to compare the means of k groups ($k \geq 2$) on some dependent measure. In particular, the null hypothesis to be tested is

$$H_0: \mu_1 = \mu_2 = \ldots = \mu_k$$

where μ_j is the population mean of the jth group. In other words, the null hypothesis is that all k groups have the same population mean. The alternative hypothesis (H_A) is that at least one of the groups has a population mean different from the others. Notice that it is not necessary for every group to differ in order for H_0 to be false; instead, it is only required that one of the groups be different.

What is the relationship between the null hypothesis being tested in ANOVA and the null hypothesis being tested in MANOVA? In the multivariate case, scores have been obtained for each subject on several dependent measures. For purposes of generality, we will let p represent the number of dependent variables in the study. Before writing the multivariate null hypothesis, we need to develop some notation. We will let μ_{mj} represent the population mean on variable m for group j. Notice that m ranges from 1 to p, while j ranges from 1 to k. Now the multivariate null hypothesis can be written as

$$H_0: \begin{matrix} \mu_{11} = \mu_{12} = \ldots = \mu_{1k} \\ \mu_{21} = \mu_{22} = \ldots = \mu_{ak} \\ \cdot \quad \cdot \quad \cdot \quad \cdot \\ \cdot \quad \cdot \quad \cdot \quad \cdot \\ \cdot \quad \cdot \quad \cdot \quad \cdot \\ \mu_{p1} = \mu_{p2} = \ldots = \mu_{pk} \end{matrix}$$

In words, the null hypothesis is that for each variable all k groups have the same population mean. The null hypothesis can be written much more compactly by using matrix algebra notation. Specifically, we can let μ_j be a column vector of population means for group j: i.e.,

$$\mu_j = \begin{bmatrix} \mu_{1j} \\ \mu_{2j} \\ \cdot \\ \cdot \\ \cdot \\ \mu_{pj} \end{bmatrix}$$

Then we can write the multivariate null hypothesis simply as an equality of vectors:

$$H_0: \mu_1 = \mu_2 = \ldots = \mu_k$$

Notice that we have not changed the meaning of H_0 in any way; instead, we have just written it more compactly. The alternative hypothesis in this case is that for at least one variable, there is at least one group with a population mean different from the others. Much like the univariate case, all it takes is one inequality in the population to make the null hypothesis false.

Univariate Test of Significance

In practice, a sample of data is randomly obtained from each of the k groups in order to decide whether or not the null hypothesis should be rejected. The univariate procedure will again be reviewed in the process of developing the multivariate test. The approach that we will take is based on the principle of model comparisons (see Cramer, 1972; Neter and Wasserman, 1974). We will use the hypothetical data in Table 2.1 first to illustrate this principle in the univariate case, and then show how it can be generalized to the multivariate case. Although in practice a larger sample size than we have here is advisable, we have chosen to present a small data set so as to facilitate computations.

Table 2.1 contains data for 5 individuals on 2 variables in each of 3 groups. Let us first perform a univariate ANOVA on the first variable, completely ignoring the second variable. According to the model comparisons principle, the first step in deriving such a test is to form a "full model." For ANOVA, a full model stipulates that an individual's score

TABLE 2.1
Hypothetical Data for Three Groups
and Two Dependent Variables

Raw Data

Group	Indiv	Y_1	Y_2
1	1	8	60
1	2	7	57
1	3	13	65
1	4	15	63
1	5	12	60
2	1	15	62
2	2	16	66
2	3	11	61
2	4	12	63
2	5	16	68
3	1	17	52
3	2	20	59
3	3	23	59
3	4	19	58
3	5	21	62

**Summary Data for the Original Variables
and the Discriminant Variates**

Group	Y_1		Y_2		V_1		V_2	
	mean	*sd*	*mean*	*sd*	*mean*	*sd*	*mean*	*sd*
1	11.0	3.4	61.0	3.1	19.5	1.1	14.9	1.1
2	14.0	2.3	64.0	2.9	19.1	0.9	15.9	0.9
3	20.0	2.2	58.0	3.7	13.3	1.0	15.3	1.0

depends solely on the group to which he or she belongs. All other causes are considered to be error. Thus, a univariate full model is given by

$$Y_{ij} = \mu_j + \epsilon_{ij}$$

where Y_{ij} is the score for subject i in group j, μ_j is the population mean of group j, and ϵ_{ij} is an error term for this subject. According to the null hypothesis, however, this model is overly complex, because if H_0 is true, we know that

$$\mu_1 = \mu_2 = \ldots = \mu_k$$

In this case, an equally good model (i.e., the models are equivalent in the population) is given by

$$Y_{ij} = \mu + \epsilon_{ij}$$

where μ is the common population mean of all of the groups. This second model is referred to as a "reduced model."

The task at this point is to choose between the full and reduced models as a description of the population. The model comparisons approach proceeds by using the principle of least squares to estimate the parameters of each model. In ANOVA models, the least squares estimate of a population mean is given by the corresponding sample mean. Thus, in the full model the estimated population mean for group j simply equals the sample mean for group j. In symbols,

$$\hat{\mu}_j = \overline{Y}_j$$

where the carat (^) over μ_j indicates an estimate of the parameter. In the reduced model,

$$\hat{\mu} = \overline{Y}.$$

where $\overline{Y}.$ is the grand mean of all of the observations regardless of group. Thus, the full ANOVA model predicts that each subject's score will equal the mean score for that subject's group, while the reduced ANOVA model predicts that each subject's score will equal the grand mean.

The full and reduced models can be compared by considering the magnitudes of the errors in each model. The estimated error for subject i in group j is simply the difference between that subject's actual score and the score predicted by the model. For example, the equation for the full model can be written as

$$\epsilon_{ij} = Y_{ij} - \mu_j$$

An estimate of the error for subject i in group j is given by

$$\hat{\epsilon}_{ij} (F) = Y_{ij} - \hat{\mu}_j = Y_{ij} - \overline{Y}_j$$

For the reduced model,

$$\hat{\epsilon}_{ij} (R) = Y_{ij} - \hat{\mu} = Y_{ij} - \overline{Y}.$$

TABLE 2.2
Errors for Full and Reduced Models for Data of Table 1

Grp	Indiv	Full Model					Reduced Model				
		e_1	e_2	e_1^2	e_2^2	e_1e_2	e_1	e_2	e_1^2	e_2^2	e_1e_2
1	1	−3	−1	9	1	3	−7	−1	49	1	7
	2	−4	−4	16	16	16	−8	−4	64	16	32
	3	2	4	4	16	8	−2	4	4	16	−8
	4	4	2	16	4	8	0	2	0	4	0
	5	1	−1	1	1	−1	−3	−1	9	1	3
	Sum	0	0	46	38	34	−20	0	126	38	34
2	1	1	−2	1	4	−2	0	1	0	1	0
	2	2	2	4	4	4	1	5	1	25	5
	3	−3	−3	9	9	9	−4	0	16	0	0
	4	−2	−1	4	1	2	−3	2	9	4	−6
	5	2	4	4	16	8	1	7	1	49	7
	Sum	0	0	22	34	21	−5	15	27	79	6
3	1	−3	−6	9	36	18	2	−9	4	81	−18
	2	0	1	0	1	0	5	−2	25	4	−10
	3	3	1	9	1	3	8	−2	64	4	−16
	4	−1	0	1	0	0	4	−3	16	9	−12
	5	1	4	1	16	4	6	1	36	1	6
	Sum	0	0	20	54	25	25	−15	145	99	−50
Grand sum		0	0	88	126	80	0	0	298	216	−10

Table 2.2 displays the errors associated with the data of Table 2.1 for both models and for both dependent variables. For each subject, e_1 represents the estimated error (ε_{jj}) for the first dependent variable, and e_2 represents the estimated error for the second dependent variable. Remember the goal is to compare the adequacy of the full and reduced models as descriptions of the data. Obviously, a good model should lead to "small" errors. An index of the magnitude of error for a model is given by the sum of squared errors for the model:

$$\text{SSE (full)} = \sum_j \sum_i \hat{\varepsilon}_{ij}^2 \text{ (F)} = \sum_j \sum_i (Y_{ij} - \overline{Y}_j)^2$$
$$\text{SSE (reduced)} = \sum_j \sum_i \hat{\varepsilon}_{ij}^2 \text{ (R)} = \sum_j \sum_i (Y_{ij} - \overline{Y}.)^2$$

In ANOVA terminology, SSE (full) is usually referred to as the sum of squares within groups, SSw, because it reflects the sum of squared errors, where error is defined for each group on the basis of its individual mean. Similarly, SSE (reduced) is called the total sum of squares, SS_T. The difference $SS_T - SS_W$ is the between group sum of squares and can be shown to equal

$$SS_B = n_j \, (\overline{Y}_j - \overline{Y}.)^2$$

where n_j is the number of subjects in group j. An F test of the null hypothesis is then given by

$$F(k - 1, N - k) = \frac{SS_B/k - 1}{SS_W/N - k}$$

where $N = \Sigma n_j$ is the total sample size. The numerator degrees of freedom (df) for the F distribution equals k-1, and the denominator df equals N-k.

Inspection of Table 2.2 shows that for the data of Table 2.1

	1st variable	2nd variable
SSE(F)	46 + 22 + 20 = 88	38 + 34 + 54 = 126
SSE(R)	126 + 27 + 145 = 298	38 + 79 + 99 = 216

Thus, the univariate F values equal

1st variable	2nd variable
$F = \dfrac{(298 - 88)/2}{88/12}$	$F = \dfrac{(216 - 126)/2}{126/12}$
$= 14.32$	$= 4.29$

By looking in a table of the F distribution, we discover that the critical F for 2 and 12 degrees of freedom and an alpha level of .05 is 3.89. Thus, there is a statistically significant difference at the .05 level between the groups for each variable considered separately.

However, for reasons discussed earlier, it might be preferable to employ a multivariate test, in order to consider the two dependent variables simultaneously. The multivariate approach accomplishes the simultaneous consideration of the variables through the use of matrix algebra. Only a brief, nonmathematical coverage will be provided here.

For further details, such textbooks as Bock (1975), Finn (1974), Harris (1975), Marascuilo and Levin (1983), Morrison (1976), Tatsuoka (1971), and Timm (1975) may be consulted.

Multivariate Test of Significance

As we have seen, the univariate test is based on a comparison of SS_B and SS_W for the particular variable. The multivariate test considers not just SS_B and SS_W for the two dependent variables (or, in general, p variables), but also the relationship between the variables. This relationship is captured in the product of e_1 times e_2 for each model (see Table 2.2). Whereas the univariate approach compares $\sum_j \sum_i e_1$ (F) versus $\sum_j \sum_i e_1$ (R) for variable 1 (and a similar comparison for variable 2), the multivariate approach also compares $\sum_j \sum_i e_1 e_2$ (F) versus $\sum_j \sum_i e_1 e_2$ (R).

Two points merit further consideration. First, what meaning can be attached to $\sum_j \sum_i e_1 e_2$, which is called a sum of cross-products? Recall that an error is just a deviation from a mean; specifically, for the full model, the error is a deviation from the group mean, whereas for the reduced model, the error is a deviation from the grand mean. The $\sum_j \sum_i e_1 e_2$ term for a model is closely related to the correlation between the 2 variables. In particular,

$$r_{Y_1 Y_2} \text{ (within groups)} = \sum_j \sum_i e_1 e_2 \,(F) / (\sum_j \sum_i e_1^2 \,(F) \sum_j \sum_i e_2^2 \,(F))^{\frac{1}{2}}$$

and

$$r_{Y_1 Y_2} \text{ (total sample)} = \sum_j \sum_i e_1 e_2 \,(R) / (\sum_j \sum_i e_1^2 \,(R) \sum_j \sum_i e_2^2 \,(R))^{\frac{1}{2}}$$

where the first correlation is a pooled (i.e., average) within-groups correlation between the two variables, and the second correlation is a measure of relationship ignoring group membership. In general, these two correlations are different, as can be seen by examining Figure 2.1, which depicts the data of Table 2.1 graphically using the horizontal axis to represent the first variable and the vertical axis to represent the second. Each ♦ in the figure represents a member of Group 1, and so forth. From inspecting the figure, it is obvious that within each group the two variables are strongly positively correlated. This is verified numerically, because

$$r_{Y_1 Y_2} \text{ (within)} = 80/((88)(126))^{\frac{1}{2}} = 0.76$$

However, if the figure is conceptualized as a representation of 15 data points irrespective of group, visual inspection suggests little or no relationship. Once again this is verified numerically, because

$$r_{Y_1 Y_2} \text{ (total)} = -10/((298)(216))^{\frac{1}{2}} = -0.04$$

Second, now that we realize the meaning of the sum of cross-products, how can this quantity be incorporated into a test statistic? Whereas in univariate ANOVA we compare the relative magnitudes of two numbers, namely SS_B and SS_W, in MANOVA the comparison is based on two matrices. To see how this is done, consider first the errors of the full model. We can represent $\sum_j \sum_i e_1^2(F)$, $\sum_j \sum_i e_1^2(F)$, and $\sum_j \sum_i e_1 e_2(F)$ in matrix form as

$$E = \begin{bmatrix} \sum_j \sum_i e_1^2(F) & \sum_j \sum_i e_1 e_2(F) \\ \sum_j \sum_i e_1 e_2(F) & \sum_j \sum_i e_2^2(F) \end{bmatrix}$$

This matrix is referred to as a sum of squares and cross-products (SSCP) matrix, and is closely related to a covariance matrix and a correlation matrix. (Dividing each element of E by N-k would yield a covariance matrix. Corresponding correlations could be found by dividing each covariance by the product of the square roots of the variances of the two variables.) Similarly, for the reduced model information regarding the errors can be written in matrix form as

$$T = \begin{bmatrix} \sum_j \sum_i e_1^2(R) & \sum_j \sum_i e_1 e_2(R) \\ \sum_j \sum_i e_1 e_2(R) & \sum_j \sum_i e_2^2(R) \end{bmatrix}$$

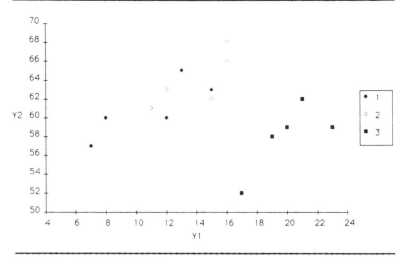

Figure 2.1

The difference between the two models can be represented as the difference between the T and E matrices. The resulting matrix, usually represented H for hypothesis sum of squares and cross-product matrix (or sometimes B for between matrix), is thus given by

$$H = T - E$$

It can be shown that in the general case of k groups and $p = 2$ variables, H equals

$$H = \begin{bmatrix} \sum_j n_j (\bar{Y}_{1j} - \bar{Y}_1.)^2 & \sum_j n_j (\bar{Y}_{1j} - \bar{Y}_1.)(\bar{Y}_{2j} - \bar{Y}_2.) \\ \sum_j n_j (\bar{Y}_{1j} - \bar{Y}_1.)(\bar{Y}_{2j} - \bar{Y}_2.) & \sum_j n_j (\bar{Y}_{2j} - \bar{Y}_2.)^2 \end{bmatrix}$$

The elements on the main diagonal are just the between-group sum of squares for each variable, while the off-diagonal element represents the between-group relationship between the two variables.

How can these matrices be used to test the multivariate null hypothesis of group equality? In the univariate case it was possible to divide SS_B

by SS_w, and with proper adjustment for degrees of freedom, arrive at an exact F value. Not surprisingly, in the multivariate case things are more complicated. The matrix analog to division of numbers is to multiply one matrix by the inverse of the other matrix. Here, then, it is necessary to multiply H by the inverse of the E matrix. This product is written as $E^{-1}H$, where E^{-1} denotes the inverse of E. In the special case of $p = 1$ (i.e., 1 dependent variable), this is simply SS_B/SS_W. In general, however, the result is a $p \times p$ matrix.

Before proceeding, it may be helpful to illustrate these concepts with the data of Table 2.1. The E, T, and H matrices for these data are given by:

$$E = \begin{bmatrix} 88 & 80 \\ 80 & 126 \end{bmatrix}$$

$$T = \begin{bmatrix} 298 & -10 \\ -10 & 216 \end{bmatrix}$$

and

$$H = \begin{bmatrix} 210 & -90 \\ -90 & 90 \end{bmatrix}$$

Multiplying H by the inverse of E yields

$$E^{-1}H = \begin{bmatrix} 7.18 & -3.95 \\ -5.27 & 3.23 \end{bmatrix}$$

Role of Discriminant Function Variates

Unlike the univariate situation, where a single ratio (i.e., SS_B/SS_W adjusted for degrees of freedom) can be used to test the null hypothesis, in the multivariate case the test of statistical significance is based on the entire $E^{-1}H$ matrix. We are obviously facing a complex situation here, because the $E^{-1}H$ matrix consists of p^2 elements. Even when p is only 2, it is not at all clear how we might interpret this many numbers to arrive at a judgment of statistical significance. It turns out, however, that we can simplify the problem through an alternate conceptualization involving certain linear combinations of the variables. Specifically, as mentioned in Section 1, the MANOVA test of significance can be viewed in terms of a set of variates often called discriminant function variates, each of which represents a linear combination of the original variables. The first such variate, which we will label V_1, is that linear combination of the original variables that has the property that SS_B/SS_W is maximized on V_1. In other words, SS_B/SS_W is less for any other linear combination of the original variables. The formation of this linear combination is equivalent to the creation of a new reference axis in Figure 2.1. That is, a new dimension is defined in the original p– dimensional space in such a way that group differences are maximized on this dimension (see Tatsuoka, 1980, for more details). Whenever $k \geq 3$ and $p \geq 2$, it is possible to find a second variate (i.e., dimension) that accounts for some between-group variation left unexplained by the first variate. (As will be discussed later, the magnitude of variation accounted for by this second variate may or may not be statistically significant.) The second such variate, V_2, maximizes SS_B/SS_W subject to the constraint that scores on V_2 be uncorrelated with scores on V_1. In general, for k groups and p variables, the total number of such variates that may be formed equals the smaller of k–1 and p. This number of variates, which we will represent by s, completely accounts for all of the between-group variation in the sample.

When $p = 2$ as in our numerical example, the general form of V_1 is given by

$$V_1 = a_{11}Y_1 + a_{21}Y_2$$

where Y_1 and Y_2 are the original variables, and a_{11} and a_{21}, are the coefficients defining V_1 in terms of the original Y variables. Similarly, V_2 is defined as

$$V_2 = a_{12}Y_1 + a_{22}Y_2$$

The values of the coefficients are found from the eigenvectors of the $E^{-1}H$ matrix. Readers interested in the methods for calculating eigenvectors should consult such sources as Green and Carroll (1976) or

Namboodiri (1984). For our purposes, we will simply state that the two eigenvectors of $E^{-1}H$ for our numerical example are

$$\begin{bmatrix} -.5538 \\ .4200 \end{bmatrix} \quad \text{and} \quad \begin{bmatrix} .1258 \\ .2211 \end{bmatrix}$$

(In fact, these vectors are only determined up to a constant of proportionality, but this is unimportant for our purposes.) This tells us that for our data, V_1 and V_2 are defined as

$$V_1 = -.5538Y_1 + .4200Y_2$$

and

$$V_2 = .1258Y_1 + .2211Y_2$$

Thus, the largest difference among the 3 groups occurs on a variate that is essentially the difference between the Y_2 and Y_1 variables.

Suppose we were to calculate V_1 and V_2 for each subject, and then form E, T, and H matrices for these variables, using the same formulas we previously used for the Ys. If we were to do this for our data, we would find (the interested reader is urged to verify these results)

$$E = \begin{bmatrix} 12 & 0 \\ 0 & 12 \end{bmatrix}$$

$$T = \begin{bmatrix} 134.148 & 0.000 \\ 0.000 & 14.716 \end{bmatrix}$$

and

$$H = \begin{bmatrix} 122.148 & 0.000 \\ 0.000 & 2.716 \end{bmatrix}$$

Several points need to be made here. First, notice that E, T, and H are all diagonal matrices (this means that all of the elements off the main diagonal equal zero). These zero off-diagonal elements reflect the fact that V_1 and V_2 are uncorrelated, within groups, between groups, and in the total sample. This fact, which is true regardless of p and k (Bock, 1975: 405) simplifies our interpretation considerably. Second, notice that each diagonal element of H equals SS_B for a given variate, while each diagonal element of E equals SS_w for that same variate. Thus, in our numerical example, the ratio of SS_B to SS_w equals $122.148/12 = 10.179$ for V_1 and $2.716/12 = 0.226$ for V_2. Third, by forming the Vs, we no longer have to consider all p^2 elements of $E^{-1}H$, because the off-diagonal elements of $E^{-1}H$ for the Vs are necessarily zero. Thus, for the variates, only the diagonal elements of $E^{-1}H$ are nonzero, and each diagonal value equals the ratio of SS_B to SS_w for that variate, as shown by $H^{-1}E$ for our data:

$$E^{-1}H = \begin{bmatrix} 10.179 & 0.000 \\ 0.000 & 0.226 \end{bmatrix}$$

In addition, it is clear that the larger these s different ratios are, the stronger is the evidence that the population means of the groups differ. Thus, we have reduced a complicated problem involving p^2 elements of a matrix to a question of how large s different ratios are. In our data, then, the question to be answered is whether the values of 10.179 and .226 are large enough that the null hypothesis should be rejected.

Before answering this question, we first need to examine the two values of 10.179 and .226 more closely. It turns out that these numbers are the eigenvalues associated with the eigenvectors of the $E^{-1}H$ matrix for the original Y variables. We mention this for two reasons: First, individuals studying multivariate statistics will repeatedly encounter eigenvalues. In MANOVA an eigenvalue of $E^{-1}H$ is simply a ratio of SS_B to SS_w for a particular discriminant function variate. Thus, larger eigenvalues indicate larger group differences on that variate. (Readers should be cautioned that some books present eigenvalues of HT^{-1}, which reflects SS_B/SS_T for a variate.) Second, we found each ratio (eigenvalue) by first calculating each subject's score on the discriminant variate and then taking the ratio of SS_B to SS_w for that variate. However, in fact, it is possible to find the eigenvalues directly from the $E^{-1}H$ matrix of the original variables. Readers interested in computations of eigenvalues should consult such references as Green and Carroll (1976) or Namboodiri (1984).

Multivariate Test Statistics

The next step in testing the multivariate null hypothesis is to ascertain how large the s eigenvalues are. In other words, we must compare their values to what we would expect to occur if the null hypothesis is true. It turns out that there are 4 reasonable ways of combining the information in the s eigenvalues, and each of these ways leads to a unique test statistic. We will present the formula for all 4 test statistics together with a brief intuitive rationale for its meaning. We will follow standard notation by letting λ_i represent the ith eigenvalue of $E^{-1}H$. Notice then that λ_i refers to the ratio of SS_B to SS_w for V_1, which is the variate for which this ratio is a maximum.

The four multivariate test statistics are Wilks' lambda, the Pillai-Bartlett trace, Roy's greatest characteristic root, and the Hotelling-Lawley trace. The formula for Wilks' lambda is

$$U = \prod_{i=1}^{s} \frac{1}{1 + \lambda_i}$$

For readers unfamiliar with the Π notation, this is a shorthand notation for multiplication in exactly the same way that Σ is an abbreviation for addition. Recalling that λ_i is SS_B/SS_W for V_i, it follows that $1/(1 + \lambda_i)$ equals SS_W/SS_T for V_i. Thus, Wilks' lambda is the product of the unexplained variances on each of the discriminant variates. As we will see shortly, small values of U lead to statistical significance. The formula for the Pillai-Bartlett trace is given by

$$V = \sum_{i=1}^{s} \frac{\lambda_i}{1 + \lambda_i}$$

It can be shown that $\lambda_i/(1 + \lambda_i)$ equals SS_B/SS_T (i.e., the proportion of explained variance) for V_i. Thus, the Pillai-Bartlett trace is the sum of explained variances on the discriminant variates. The formula for Roy's greatest characteristic root is

$$GCR = \frac{\lambda_1}{1 + \lambda_1}$$

which is SS_B/SS_T for V_1 alone. Thus, Roy's test is based only on the first discriminant variate. Finally, the formula for the Hotelling-Lawley trace is

$$T = \sum_{i=1}^{s} \lambda_i$$

which is the sum of SS_B/SS_W for each of the discriminant variates.

Any of these 4 statistics might be used to test the multivariate null hypothesis. Only in the special case of $s = 1$ (i.e., either $k = 2$ or $p = 1$) do the 4 approaches necessarily agree with one another.

Whenever $s > 1$, it is possible that the 4 approaches will disagree as to whether the null hypothesis should be rejected at a specified alpha level. Choosing which test to employ involves a complex consideration of robustness and statistical power. Olson (1976, 1979) and Stevens (1979) have provided an enlightening discussion of the relevant issues.

We will only present the tests of significance based on U (Wilks' lambda) and V (Pillai-Bartlett trace), because the former is historically the most widely used of the 4 approaches and the latter was found to be the most robust by Olson (1976). For further information on R and T, the reader is referred to Harris (1975) and Olson (1976).

Recalling that for the data in Table 2.1 the eigenvalues of $E^{-1}H$ were $\lambda_1 = 10.179$ and $\lambda_2 = 0.226$, it easily follows that U = 0.0729 and V = 1.0951. Based on either statistic, should the null hypothesis be rejected? To answer this question, the observed value of the test statistic must be compared to the sampling distribution of the statistic under the null hypothesis. The sampling distributions of both U and V are exceedingly complex. For this reason, approximations to the sampling distribution are usually employed. For Wilks' lambda, Rao (1951) showed that a complicated transformation of the U statistic results in a variable with an approximate F distribution. The specific transformation, which is performed by most computer programs, alleviating the need for hand calculation, is given by

$$R = \frac{(1 - U^{1/q})\ (mq - \frac{1}{2}p\ (k - 1) + 1)}{U^{1/q}\ p^{(k-1)}}$$

where

$$m = N - 1 - (1/2)\ (p + K)$$

and

$$q = \sqrt{\frac{p^2 (k-1)^2 - 4}{p^2 + (k-1)^2 - 5}}$$

The R statistic (not to be confused with Roy's greatest characteristic root) is distributed approximately as an F variable with $p(k-1)$ and $mq-1/2p(k-1) + 1$ degrees of freedom. Whenever $k = 2$ or $k = 3$ (regardless of p) or $p = 1$ or $p = 2$ (regardless of k), R is distributed exactly as an F variable (assuming that the required statistical assumptions to be discussed later are met). A simpler transformation is necessary for the V statistic:

$$F \approx \frac{(N-k-p+s)\,V}{b(s-V)}$$

where $b = \max (k-1, p)$. Pillai (1960) showed that this transformation of V has an approximate F distribution with sb and $s(N-k-p+s)$ degrees of freedom. For the data in Table 2.1, then, tests are obtained by substituting U and V into the corresponding formulas. For Wilks' lambda, this yields R = 14.864, which implies a p-value of .00003 in an F distribution with 4 and 22 degrees of freedom. For the Pillai-Bartlett trace, the observed F equals 7.261, which corresponds to a p-value of .00079 with 4 and 24 degrees of freedom. Thus, with either test statistic, the null hypothesis is rejected at the .05 level.

Comparison of MANOVA and ANOVA

Now that we have presented the omnibus significance tests in ANOVA and MANOVA, let us consider the following examples to further compare the univariate and multivariate approaches. Figures 2.2a and 2.2b present graphical representations of hypothetical data, similar to Figure 2.1, which represented the data of Table 2.1. However, instead of representing each individual subject in the figure as was done in Figure 2.1, ellipses are used in Figures 2.2a and 2.2b to represent the central 95% of subjects in each group. Figure 2.2a represents data comparing a treatment group designed to alleviate hypertension with a control group, where the two dependent variables are systolic and

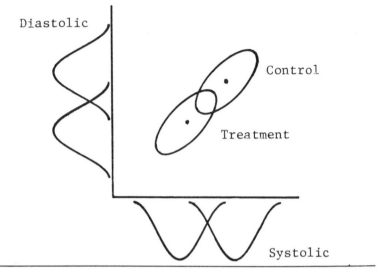

Figure 2.2a

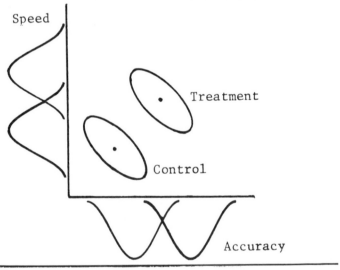

Figure 2.2b

diastolic blood pressure. Figure 2.2b represents data comparing a treatment group to a control group on a choice reaction time task in cognitive psychology, where the dependent variables are accuracy and speed of response. These two figures are drawn in such a way that the univariate statistics are the same in both situations. This can be seen from the figures by examining the distributions projected onto the axes representing the two variables. However, when the variables are considered jointly, the groups in Figure 2.2b are more separable than the groups in Figure 2.2a. This distinction arises because in the first figure the two dependent variables are positively correlated within groups, while in the second figure the correlation is negative. As previously illustrated, a basic difference between the multivariate test and separate univariate tests is that only the multivariate test is sensitive to the direction and magnitude of the correlations among the dependent variables. Thus, although univariate tests of data from Figure 2.2a would yield identical results to univariate tests for 2.2b (because the means are the same on both variables in both cases), the multivariate test would be different. As might be expected, the multivariate test would judge the groups to be more different from one another in Figure 2.2b than in Figure 2.2a.

Although it is obvious geometrically from the figures that the groups overlap less in Figure 2.2b than in 22.2a when the variables are considered simultaneously, it may be less obvious why the correlation between the variables is so important. To consider this issue, suppose for simplicity that in each experiment subjects have been randomly assigned to groups. In spite of random assignment, the samples will inevitably differ to some degree because of sampling error. For example, the most severe hypertensives might have been assigned to the control group. If, in fact, this occurred and the null hypothesis is true, we would expect the control group to have a higher mean than the experimental group on both dependent variables, because the two variables are positively correlated. The situation in the second experiment (Figure 2.2b) is very different. Suppose here that by chance more accurate subjects were assigned to the treatment group. If, in fact, this occurred and the null hypothesis is true, we would expect the treatment group to have a higher mean than the control group on accuracy but a lower mean than the control group on speed, because the two variables are negatively correlated within a group. According to the figure, however, the experimental group has the higher mean on both variables. Such an occurrence is extremely unlikely due to sampling error alone, because sampling error here would make one group higher on one variable but lower on the other. The fact that the experimental group has a higher mean for both variables is strong evidence for a nonzero treatment effect. Thus, the group differences depicted in Figure 2.2b are less likely to arise from sampling error than are the differences depicted in Figure 2.2a.

There are two important points to note from this example. First, correlations between variables are important in judging the magnitude of group differences. MANOVA has a distinct advantage over ANOVA in this regard. Second, although statistically significant effects can be obtained when the data resemble Figure 2.2a, the multivariate test is less powerful than it would be for the data depicted in Figure 2.2b.

When the multivariate omnibus null hypothesis is rejected, all that can be said is that it is not true that

$$\mu_1 = \mu_2 \ldots = \mu_k$$

Obviously, more work is necessary to interpret the meaning of group differences on the set of variables. A variety of procedures exist for further probing the meaning of a statistically significant MANOVA result. The majority of this monograph will be devoted to precisely this topic. Before considering interpretational issues, however, we will touch briefly on four other topics regarding the omnibus test: assumptions, robustness, power, and measures of effect size.

Assumptions of MANOVA

As with any inferential statistical technique, the mathematics of MANOVA is based on a set of assumptions. In particular, the assumptions needed for MANOVA closely parallel those for ANOVA. The MANOVA assumptions are

(1) Units (e.g., persons, families, countries) are randomly sampled from the population of interest.

(2) Observations are statistically independent of one another.

(3) The dependent variables have a multivariate normal distribution within each group. In practice, this can usually be thought of as a requirement that each separate variable follow a normal distribution. In theory, however, univariate normality is necessary but not sufficient for multivariate normality (Carroll, 1961).

(4) The k groups have a common within-group population covariance matrix. This assumption is twofold: (1) The ANOVA homogeneity of variance assumption must be met for each dependent variable; (2) the correlation between any two dependent variables must be the same in all k groups.

Robustness of MANOVA

Although the aforementioned assumptions are mathematical requirements for MANOVA, in practice it is unlikely that all of the assumptions will be met precisely. Fortunately, as in ANOVA, at least under many conditions, violating the assumptions does not necessarily invalidate the results. In other words, both ANOVA and MANOVA are relatively robust to violations of the assumptions in many circumstances. Although less is known about robustness for MANOVA than for ANOVA, the general pattern of results is very similar. In particular, MANOVA is not robust to violations of either of the first two assumptions.

A number of Monte Carlo studies (e.g., Ito, 1969; Mardia, 1971; Olson, 1974) have been conducted to investigate the extent to which MANOVA is robust to violations of multivariate normality and equality of covariance matrices. It is important to realize here that "MANOVA" can actually be any of four things, because of the four different test statistics. Indeed, the relative robustness and power of each test statistic (to be discussed next) are the relevant criteria for choosing which statistic to use.

Departures from multivariate normality generally have only very slight effects on the Type I error rates of the four statistics. The sole known exception to this rule is that Roy's greatest characteristic root test may lead to too many Type I errors when only one of several groups has a distribution with high positive Kurtosis (Olson, 1976). As in ANOVA departures from normality may reduce statistical power. One possible solution to this problem is to employ transformations of the data to achieve normality (or at least approximate it more closely), in much the same manner as ANOVA. At the time of this writing, none of the three most popular statistical packages (BMDP, SAS, SPSS-X) contains procedures for assessing degree of departure from multivariate normality. The most promising approach at this time is a graphical test described by Johnson and Wichern (1982) and Stevens (1984), who provides an example of how the test can be conducted easily using BMDP.

The effects of failing to meet the equality of covariance matrices assumption are more complicated. When sample sizes are unequal, none of the four test statistics is robust (Hakstian et al., 1979; Ito, 1980). Depending on the relationship between the sample sizes and the covariance matrices, either too many or too few Type I errors will result. Several statisticians have developed test statistics for the situation in which covariance matrices are unequal. Timm (1975) has recommended Yao's (1965) procedure, which is a generalization of Welch's method for the univariate Behrens-Fisher problem. When sample sizes are equal, all of the test statistics tend to be robust unless sample sizes are small, or the number of variables is large, and the difference in matrices is quite large. However, Olson (1974, 1976) has found that the Pillai-Bartlett trace is much more robust across a wide range of population configurations than any of the other three statistics. Olson (1979) and Stevens (1979) have argued the practical implication of this finding for choosing an optimal test statistic. In general, with equal sample sizes, the Pillai-Bartlett trace seems to be the best of the 4 multivariate test statistics in terms of Type I error, because it is most robust to violations of assumptions. However, it should be realized that even the Pillai-Bartlett trace is not robust to violation of equality of covariance matrices when sample sizes are unequal. Although a test of homogeneity of covariance matrices is widely available (Box's M), this test is generally not useful, because the test itself is extremely sensitive to departures from normality (Olson, 1974).

Statistical Power

Issues of statistical power (the probability of rejecting the null hypothesis when it is false) are just as relevant for MANOVA as for ANOVA. However, a priori estimation of power when planning a MANOVA study is difficult, because so many unknown parameters must be estimated. Instead of attempting to cover this complex topic in detail, we will provide a brief overview and refer the reader to the references we cite for additional detail.

Stevens (1980) has written a useful article on MANOVA power aimed at social science researchers. Several general findings emerge from Stevens's work. First, as p (the number of dependent variables) increases, it is necessary to increase sample size to maintain a given level of power for a specified effect size. Thus, it is wise to limit the number of dependent variables to a reasonably small number (e.g., 10 or fewer) unless sample sizes are quite large. Second, "the power of the multivariate tests with small-to-moderate group and effect sizes is poor, as is true in univariate ANOVA" (Stevens, 1980: 736). Third, "the magnitude of within-group intercorrelations definitely has an effect on power" (1980: 736). Indeed, researchers often do not realize that depending on these intercorrelations, the MANOVA test can be either much more powerful or much less powerful than the separate ANOVA tests on individual variables. This differential power explains the seemingly anomalous situation in which the MANOVA test is significant but none of the ANOVAs is, or the opposite situation, in which the MANOVA is nonsignificant but some or even all of the ANOVAs are significant. Ramsey (1982) has thoroughly compared the relative powers of MANOVA and separate ANOVAs in the two-group case.

Stevens (1980) provides tables for calculating power in both the two-group and the k-group case. However, the tables for the k-group case leave many gaps, as Stevens admits. Muller and Peterson (1984) describe a procedure whereby a linear models program can be used to calculate multivariate power even in the k-group case. Olson (1976, 1979) and Stevens (1979) discuss conditions that favor the 4 different multivariate test statistics in terms of power. When the noncentrality structure is "concentrated" (i.e., groups differ along a single dimension), the power ordering (from most to least powerful) of the 4 test statistics is R, T, W, and V. However, when the noncentrality structure is "diffuse" (the groups differ along several dimensions), the power ordering is V, W, T, and R. Thus, no multivariate test statistic is uniformly most powerful. Finally, Pruzek has offered a useful recommendation for one way to increase power regardless of which test statistic is used. Pruzek (1971: 187) argues that often it is advisable "to combine (usually add) highly similar response measures in MANOVA studies, particularly when basic measurements tend individually to be quite unreliable.... When the correlations among the set of dependent variables differ widely, principles and methodology of factor analysis seem likely to offer hope of facilitating interpretations of data." We will discuss this further in Section 3.

Measures of Effect Size

Suppose a researcher has obtained a statistically significant multivariate result in testing an omnibus null hypothesis. As in ANOVA, a statistically significant result is not necessarily an important result, because trivial differences may be statistically significant with huge sample sizes. On the other hand, meaningful sample differences may go undetected when sample sizes are small. A number of multivariate strength of association measures that are independent of sample size have been proposed in the literature. Cramer and Nicewander (1979) provide a review of these measures.

In univariate ANOVA, one measure of strength of association between group membership and a dependent variable is the correlation ratio, usually represented by $\hat{\eta}^2$. Eta squared ($\hat{\eta}^2$) is defined to be

$$\hat{\eta}^2 = SS_B/(SS_B + SS_W)$$

It can be shown that eta squared is equal to the squared multiple correlation between the dependent variable and $k - 1$ dummy variables coded to represent group membership. In MANOVA the analog to a multiple correlation is a canonical correlation (see Knapp, 1978; Thompson, forthcoming). In a k-group, p-variable MANOVA there are s canonical correlations (where, again, $s = \min (k = 1, p)$). It can be shown that the following relationship holds relating a canonical correlation (r_i) to an eigenvalue of $E^{-1}H$ (λ_i):

$$R_i = \frac{\lambda_i}{1 + \lambda_i}$$

Cramer and Nicewander (1979) proposed as a measure of multivariate association the average of the s canonical correlations,

$$\hat{\eta}^2_{mult} = \sum_{i=1}^{s} r_i/s$$

However, recall that

$$V = \sum_{i=1}^{s} \frac{\lambda_i}{1 + \lambda_i} = \sum_{i=1}^{s} r_i$$

so that

$$\hat{\eta}^2_{mult} = V/s$$

which is just the value of the Pillai-Bartlett trace divided by s. This value is a measure of the degree of association in the sample, not the degree of association to be expected in the population (see Maxwell et al., 1981). Serlin (1982) has derived an adjusted measure that may be used to estimate the strength of association in the population:

$$\hat{\eta}^2_{mult} \ (adj) = 1 - (1 - \eta^2_{mult}) \left(\frac{N-1}{N-b-1} \right)$$

where N is total sample size and b is the larger of p and k - 1. Applying these formulas to the data of Table 2.1 yields

$$\hat{\eta}^2_{mult} = 1.0951/2 = 0.5476$$

$$\hat{\eta}^2_{mult} \ (adj) = 0.4722$$

Thus, it is estimated that 47.22% of the population variance in the two dependent measures can be attributed to group membership.

Numerical Example

The following example is provided to demonstrate the different results and interpretations gained from the various procedures we have covered thus far. The example will be used throughout the monograph to illustrate the various methods of analysis. The data come from a longitudinal study of the developmental changes in neuropsychological correlates of reading achievements (Fletcher and Satz, 1980). Given the purposes of this monograph, no attempt will be made to build a theory for the data.

The data are from 571 second-grade children in Florida schools. The classification variable consisted of a test-based assessment of word recognition skills. Four groups were formed based on standard deviation cutoffs: (1) severely disabled readers (N = 93); (2) mildly disabled readers (N = 113); (3) average readers (N = 274); and (4) superior readers (N = 91). The criterion variables for the ANOVA analyses consisted of the Peabody Picture Vocabulary Test (PPVT), Verbal Fluency Test (VF), Similarities subtest of the Wechsler Preschool and Primary Scale of Intelligence (SIM), Beery Visual Motor Integration Test (VMI),

TABLE 2.3
Means, Standard Deviations, and Within-Cells Correlations
for Real Data Example

Variable		Group				
		Overall Means	Severe N = 93	Mild N = 113	Average N = 274	Superior N = 91
PPVT	M	107.44	97.18	103.19	107.88	121.87
	SD	20.85	11.19	12.88	14.70	37.69
RD	M	13.30	11.97	13.17	13.54	14.12
	SD	1.73	1.96	1.32	1.41	2.03
EF	M	12.26	9.37	11.84	12.76	14.21
	SD	2.94	2.95	2.31	2.32	3.10
VF	M	33.73	28.39	31.85	34.31	39.74
	SD	8.73	6.97	8.03	7.69	10.12
VMI	M	86.78	74.25	83.04	89.42	96.32
	SD	18.57	11.20	17.63	17.71	20.59
SIM	M	17.48	15.55	16.97	17.79	19.18
	SD	2.41	2.94	2.29	1.97	1.50

Pooled within-cells correlations

Variable	PPVT	RD	EF	VF	VMI	SIM
PPVT	1.00					
RD	0.42	1.00				
EF	0.42	0.52	1.00			
VF	0.08	0.07	0.15	1.00		
VMI	0.04	0.22	0.32	0.09	1.00	
SIM	0.17	0.15	0.19	0.22	0.08	1.00

Recognition-Discrimination Test (RD), and the Embedded Figures Test (EF). The PPVT is a general verbal measure of IQ, whereas the VF and SIM tests are verbal criteria. The EF taps higher-order nonverbal abilities, whereas the VMI and RD are general nonverbal measures.

Table 2.3 presents the means, standard deviations, and pooled within-cell correlations for the data. In Table 2.4 are the eigenvalues and canonical correlations for the data. Notice that most of the between-group variance (93.14%) is explained by the first root. Calculating the overall MANOVA tests of significance from the eigenvalues shows that there is a statistically significant association between the classification variable and criterion variables at the .001 level for all 4 multivariate test statistics (see Table 2.4). The sample value of multivariate association equals 0.14 for these data. The corresponding adjusted population estimate equals 0.13.

TABLE 2.4
Eigenvalues and Omnibus MANOVA Tests
for Real Data Numerical Example
Eigenvalues and Canonical Correlations

Root No.	Eigenvalue		% of Variance		Canonical Correlations
1	0.61		93.14		0.61
2	0.04		6.52		0.20
3	0.00		0.34		0.05

Test Name	Value	Approx. F	Hyp df	Err df	p
Pillais V	.41997	15.30	18	1692.00	.001
Hotellings	.64997	20.25	18	1682.00	.001
Wilks' lambda	.59626	17.72	18	1590.06	.001
Roy's GCR	.37709		18		.001

Given that the omnibus tests are significant, the next step is to probe the data further to interpret the nature of the differences. There is a whole array of techniques for analyzing and interpreting significant MANOVAs. These techniques will be discussed in detail in the next two sections.

3. ANALYZING AND INTERPRETING SIGNIFICANT MANOVAS

Once a significant overall MANOVA has been found, the next step is to investigate the specific differences between groups. As in ANOVA, this involves determining which groups are responsible for the significant omnibus test. In addition, the follow-up analyses are used to evaluate which variables are important for group separation. Investigating these differences requires further analysis of both the criterion and classification variables. There are a number of techniques available and they will be discussed in detail in this section. We will also present several examples of how to apply these techniques with actual data. It is important to note that there is no one "right" method for these follow-up analyses; rather, the type of analyses performed will be determined by the research questions and type of data collected.

Analyzing Criterion Variables

UNIVARIATE F TESTS

Historically, following a significant MANOVA with ANOVAs on each of the p variables was one of the first methods recommended for interpreting group differences (Cramer and Bock, 1966). Many researchers still advocate this method, which is often referred to as the Least Significant Difference (LSD) test or the protected F or t procedure (Bock, 1975; Cooley and Lohnes, 1971; Finn, 1974; Hummel and Sligo, 1971; Spector, 1977; Wilkinson, 1975). The term "protected" comes from the idea that the overall multivariate test provides protection from an inflated alpha level on the p univariate tests. Assuming that the null hypothesis of no differences between groups is true, the overall alpha level for the p univariate tests is held near the specified nominal alpha. Hummel and Sligo (1971) demonstrated in a Monte Carlo study that investigated various numbers of criteria, sample sizes, and within-groups correlations that this protected F approach adequately controls the experimentwise error rate near the nominal alpha level. They therefore recommend this procedure as the method of choice. If *only* the univariate F tests are interpreted it is implicitly assumed that the p variables do not represent some smaller set of dimensions or factors.

Each univariate F ratio that reaches the specified alpha level is considered to be statistically significant and available for interpretation (Bock, 1975). The F tests are invariant under permutation of the other criterion measures. In other words, each F test is exactly the test that would have been obtained if it were the only dependent variable under study. Thus, the p univariate tests are insensitive to the correlations among the variables. Although the univariate F tests are insensitive to the correlations among the variables, the F tests are not statistically independent, because of the correlations. This situation is analogous to the test of nonorthogonal between-group contrasts in ANOVA. The largest single F ratio occurs for the variable that has the largest between-group difference relative to within-group variation. Likewise, the smallest F ratio represents the variable with the smallest group differences. However, correlated criterion variables do not represent independent sources of variation and should not be viewed as partial tests of the overall MANOVA test (Finn, 1974).

The protected F approach has a flaw in regard to controlling Type I error. As Miller (1966: 93) concludes, "the preliminary F test guards against falsely rejecting the null hypothesis when the null hypothesis is true. However, when, in fact, the null hypothesis is false and likely to be rejected, the second stage of the LSD gives no increased protection to that part (if any) of the null hypothesis which still remains true." In many cases the null hypothesis of no group differences is in fact false for one or more but not all variables. Hence, the multivariate test will produce significant results with a high probability if power is sufficient. However, univariate tests will then be performed for those variables for which there is no true difference as well as for those variables for which there is a difference. Because the individual alpha levels are not adjusted despite performing multiple significance tests, the overall multivariate test does not provide "protection" for each of the p univariate tests. Consequently in such cases the experimentwise error rate for the set of p univariate F ratios may be inflated above the nominal alpha level, even if the initial MANOVA test was significant. It is precisely for this reason that the protected F or LSD approach is usually considered an unacceptable method for performing post hoc comparisons in univariate ANOVA. Thus, the actual degree of alpha protection afforded by the approach is often misunderstood (Bray and Maxwell, 1982; Strahan, 1982).

An alternative to employing MANOVA to control the experimentwise alpha is to use a Bonferroni procedure (Harris, 1975). This involves dividing the nominal alpha by the number of variables in the study and comparing each individual F ratio to the critical F for this adjusted alpha level. One important question is whether this procedure is more or less powerful than the MANOVA method. There is no simple answer to this question. As mentioned in Section 2, Ramsey (1982) showed that even in the special case of two groups, the relative power is a complex function of three factors: (1) sample size, (2) the treatment effects for each of the p variables, and (3) the within-groups correlation between the variables.

In general, use of separate univariate F tests or the Bonferroni procedure ignores any relationships among the p variables. Therefore, many potentially useful sources of information, such as suppressor effects or redundancies, are left unknown. Bock (1975: 417-420) provides some excellent examples of the effects of various correlation patterns among the criteria on the univariate F tests and discriminant analysis results. However, if the purpose of the analysis is to control the Type I error rate for a set of p univariate ANOVAs, then these methods are generally appropriate. Additionally, the separate ANOVAs can provide information concerning the contribution of individual variables

TABLE 3.1
Analyses and Statistics for Hypothetical Data Set

		Dimension Reduction Analysis				
Roots	*Eigen Value*	*Wilks' lambda*	*F*	*HDF*	*EDF*	*Sig of F*
1 to 2	10.18	.073	14.86	4.00	22.00	.001
2 to 2	0.23	.815	2.60	1.00	11.50	.143

	Variables	
Statistic	Y_1	Y_2
Univariate F_S	14.32	4.29
	$p < .001$	$p < .039$
SDWs		
Function 1	−1.50	1.36
Function 2	.34	.72
CVCs		
Function 1	−.47	.22
Function 2	.88	.98
u statistic	2.96	2.43
Fs-to-remove	8.48	16.77
	$p < .001$	$p < .001$
Step-down Fs with Y_1 entered first	14.32	16.77
	$p < .001$	$p < .001$

NOTE: SDW = standardized discriminant weight; CVC = canonical variate correlation.

when used in combination with other techniques such as discriminant analysis (Finn, 1974; Borgen and Seling, 1978).

Throughout this section we will exemplify the use of the various follow-up methods with the hypothetical data set from Section 2. We will also present a complete example at the end of this section based on the real Fletcher and Satz data.

Recall that the overall multivariate test for the hypothetical data was significant, so follow-up analyses are necessary to further explain the group differences. Each of the univariate ANOVAs is significant at the .05 level (see Table 3.1). Using the Bonferroni method for determining the significance level, alpha of $\alpha/p = .05/2 = .025$, only Y_1 is significant. Y_2 is not significant using this more conservative approach.

DISCRIMINANT ANALYSIS

Discriminant analysis finds the linear combination of the *p* variables that best separates the *k* groups by maximizing the between-group variance of the linear combination relative to the within-group variance. The procedure produces s = min $(p, k - 1)$ discriminant functions, some or all of which may be significant at the specified alpha level. Each of the discriminant functions is a linear composite of the p variables that maximizes group separation with the restriction that scores on each of the functions are uncorrelated with scores on each of the preceding functions. In the special case of $k = 2$, the discriminant analysis is formally equivalent to a multiple regression problem (Tatsuoka, 1971).

In general, Huberty (1975) indicates that discriminant analysis is appropriate for four purposes: (1) separation between the k groups; (2) discrimination with respect to dimensions and variates; (3) estimation of the relationship between the p variables and k group membership variables; and (4) classifying individuals to specific populations. The first three uses are most relevant in the follow-up analysis of MANOVA.

In the context of interpreting a significant MANOVA, discriminant analysis can provide information concerning (1) the minimum number of dimensions that underlie the group differences on the p variables, (2) how the individual variables relate to the underlying dimensions and the other variables, (3) which variables are most important for group separation, and (4) how the groups can be represented geometrically in this reduced discriminant space (Borgen and Seling, 1978; Cooley and Lohnes, 1971; Fletcher et al., 1978; Huberty, 1975, 1984; Overall and Klett, 1972; Tatsuoka, 1971).

Within discriminant analysis there are several alternatives that address the above points and facilitate interpretation of the discriminant functions either separately or together. Of the s discriminant functions that result from the analysis, only those that are statistically significant are interpreted. In many cases, only a single function exists. However, in some cases several significant functions will be obtained, indicating that there are several constructs or dimensions underlying the data. Although this more accurately reflects the complexity of the data, it can also present problems in interpretation of the results.

One of the most common methods of interpreting the discriminant function is to use the discriminant function standardized weights or coefficients (Darlington et al., 1973; Huberty, 1975; Stevens, 1972; Tatsuoka, 1971). The weights are the coefficients of the linear combinations derived to maximize group separation. The coefficients represent the *relative* contribution of the variable to the discriminant function; however, the weights are highly influenced by the intercorrelations among the other variables (Bock, 1975; Finn, 1974; Timm, 1975). The standardized discriminant weights are analogous to standardized regression weights. Thus, the effects of the variables' interdependencies dramatically affect the interpretation and are not easily controlled. Just as in the interpretation of beta weights in multiple regression (Darlington, 1968), problems due to suppressor effects, multicolinearity, and variable redundancies must all be considered in the interpretation of the discriminant coefficients (Finn, 1974; Huberty, 1984; Timm, 1975; Wilkinson, 1975). Discriminant coefficients can change drastically with the addition or deletion of one or more variables.

In addition, if two variables are highly correlated with each other, the relative importance of the variables may be split between the two variables, or one variable may receive a large weight and the other a small weight (see Bock, 1975: 417-420, for examples). However, each variable may discriminate equally well when used singularly (Wilkinson, 1975). This has led several writers to caution against employing discriminant coefficients for interpretation when the p variables are highly correlated (Borgen and Selig, 1978; Finn, 1974; Huberty, 1984; Spector, 1977). Huberty (1975) also points out that discriminant coefficients have been erroneously interpreted as if they are factor loadings. In fact, the coefficients do not represent the common parts of discrimination, rather the discriminant coefficients are only *partial* coefficients. The relationship between the magnitude of a coefficient for a given variable and the univariate F ratio for the same variable may be very different (see Bock, 1975; Wilkinson, 1975), particularly when the variables are correlated. The difference is because the F ratio is calculated without regard to the other variables, while the discriminant coefficient considers the intercorrelations among the p variables (Bock, 1975).

Huberty (1984) proposes a transformation of the standardized discriminant weights as a means of controlling for multicolinearity between variables. This index is referred to as a u statistic and is given by

$$u_{ji} = (b^*_{ji})^2 / r^{ii}$$

where u_{ji} is the index of importance for variable i and function j, b^*_{ji} is the standardized discriminant weight for variable i and function j, and r^{ii} is the ith diagonal element of the inverse of the within-groups correlations matrix. Dividing by r^{ii} takes into consideration the colinearity of the variable with the other dependent variables. (See Huberty, 1984, for details of how to calculate the index.)

An alternative to interpreting the standardized discriminant coefficients is to employ a canonical structure matrix (Meredith, 1964;

Porebski, 1966a, 1966b). This procedure involves calculating the correlation of each individual variable with each discriminant function (referred to as canonical variate correlations). More specifically, the discriminant variates determined through the linear composite of the p variables are correlated with each of the original p variables. (For the mathematics, see Porebski, 1966b; Stevens, 1972; or Timm, 1975). This method provides a measure of how each of the p variables independently relates to each of the s discriminant functions. Bargmann (1970) contends that in cases in which some variables have large correlations with the discriminant function and others have small correlations, the ones with the larger correlations contribute most to group separation. This method is useful for ordering the variables as to their relative contributions to group separation. However, as in multiple regression the variables operate as a set and changing that set can have dramatic effects (Darlington, 1968; Huberty, 1975).

Some researchers recommend using the canonical variate correlations rather than using the discriminant coefficients for interpretation (Bargmann, 1970; Borgen & Seling, 1978; Cooley and Lohnes, 1971; Darlington et al., 1973; Timm, 1975). The reason given for this decision is that the correlations are supposedly more stable than the weights in cross-validation. Three separate studies investigating the stability of discriminant coefficients and canonical variate correlations found mixed results (Barcikowski and Stevens, 1975; Huberty, 1975b; Thorndike and Weiss, 1973). Thus, the alleged superiority attributed to the canonical variate correlation method (see Borgen and Selig, 1978; Cooley and Lohnes, 1971; Spector, 1977) does not hold up under empirical testing.

What many researchers do not realize is that these two approaches answer different questions. The discriminant weights, as previously stated, are analogous to regression weights, and represent the unique contribution of a variable to the composite variate. The canonical variate correlations, on the other hand, are analogous to factor loadings and, hence, represent how much variance a given variable shares with the underlying composite. For this reason, the canonical variate correlations are more useful than the discriminant weights for interpreting the *substantive* nature of the discriminant function. In contrast, the discriminant weights provide information concerning the degree of necessity of retaining a variable in the complete set of discriminators. Again it should be noted, however, that the variables operate as a set and changing that set (by adding or deleting a variable) will affect the weights of all the variables in that set.

An additional method of determining the importance of individual variables for group separation is the F-to-remove index (Huberty, 1984). This index considers all p variables simultaneously and across all of the discriminant dimensions. The F-to-remove index tests the hypothesis that the k group means are equal on a given variable when the other variables are partialled out. A large F value for a given variable indicates that deleting that variable decreases group separation substantially. The advantage of this index is that in a two-group case the F-to-remove is proportional to estimates of the decrease in the intergroup distances if that variable is deleted and it also takes into consideration the colinearity among the variables (Huberty, 1984; Huberty and Smith, 1982).

A major advantage of discriminant analysis over the protected F approach is that discriminant analysis reduces and explains the p variables in terms of s underlying dimensions. In essence, the number of significant discriminant functions denotes the underlying psychological or theoretical dimensions of the criterion variables. Investigating the dimensionality of the data is impossible with the univariate F approach because the univariate approach does not address this issue at all. With one significant function, inspection of the group means along the significant dimension for each variable characterizes group differences. If more than one discriminant function is significant, the group centroids can be plotted (geometrically) in discriminant space to facilitate interpretation (Cooley and Lohnes, 1971; Borgen and Selig, 1978; Kaplan and Litrownik, 1977; Tatsuoka, 1971). Kaplan and Litrownik (1977) provide an excellent and readable discussion of employing centroid maps to interpret MANOVAs. Using either or both the standardized coefficients or the canonical variate correlations, the dimensions may be interpreted in terms of some theoretically meaningful construct. If there are more than two significant functions, pairwise two-dimensional plots may be employed. Excellent and detailed discussions of further graphing techniques in multivariate analysis can be found in Everitt (1978) and Gnanadesikan (1977).

Although plotting the group centroids in discriminant space provides a graphical representation of the group differences, simple centroid plotting does not provide information on how the groups differ on the original p variables. Overall and Klett (1972) suggest that inserting the original measurement vectors into the reduced discriminant space more clearly illustrates how the groups differ with respect to the original p variables. Measurement vectors are determined by calculating the product-moment correlation of group means on each variable with the group means on the derived discriminant variates. The length of the vector is calculated by multiplying the between-groups correlations by the univariate F value for a given variable. The vectors are then plotted in two-dimensional discriminant space. The beginning of each vector is the grand centroid, that is the mean of all of the group means for each of the variables. Interpretation is facilitated by observing how a particular variable relates to one group centroid versus the other group centroids, while the length of the vector indicates the relative importance of each variable for group separation. Overall and Klett (1972: 292-295) discuss how to calculate and plot the measurement vectors, in addition to providing an example of their use.

Discriminant analysis provides more sophisticated and complex analyses of the data than does the univariate approach. However, this complexity can be a drawback to the use of discriminant analysis, particularly when there are multiple significant discriminant functions. The underlying dimensionality of the variables, the relationship of the variables to the underlying dimensions, and the interrelationships among the variables are all considered in discriminant analysis. In contrast, the univariate approach simply provides the individual effects of each variable, ignoring all other variables. Inspecting the univariate F ratios along with the discriminant coefficients and canonical variate correlations will often provide useful information for interpreting the unique and common contribution of each variable. It should again be noted that these methods will also produce different types of information, particularly when the variables are correlated (see Spector, 1977; Wilkinson, 1975).

The discriminant function analyses for the hypothetical data set are presented in Table 3.1. First notice that only one significant function is significant using the partitioned U method (see dimension reduction analysis in Table 3.1). This indicates that group differences on the two dependent variables can be explained by one underlying dimension. The remaining analyses indicate how to interpret this dimension. The standardized discriminant weights (SDWs) and canonical variate correlations (CVCs) both show that the first dimension is represented by the difference between the two variables. Both of these approaches, as well as the u statistics and the Fs-to-remove, also support the univariate F values by implying that both Y_1 and Y_2 are important for group separation, although Y_1 is somewhat more important according to all the indices. Notice that the Fs-to-remove are substantially higher than the

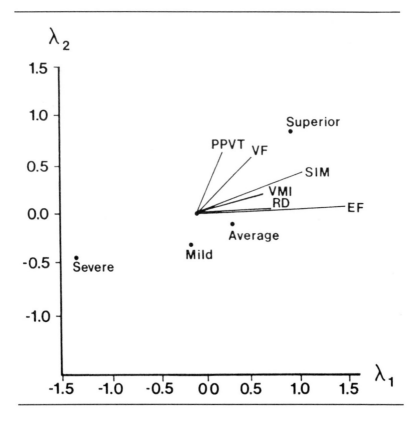

Figure 3.1

univariate Fs for both variables. This indicates that because of the correlation between the variables, each variable has a stronger effect in the context of the other than it has by itself. The plot of the group centroids (see Figure 2.1) graphically demonstrates the differences between these groups in the discriminant space. Note that all of the analyses, including the univariate Fs, indicate that both variables are important for group separation. However, the univariate Fs, CVCs, and F-to-remove statistics all suggest that Y_1 is more important than Y_2.

STEP-DOWN ANALYSIS

Step-down analysis (Roy, 1958) is a form of analysis of covariance in which the criterion variables are entered in a specified order to test the relative contribution of successive measures (Bock, 1975; Bock and Haggard, 1968; Stevens, 1972, 1973). This technique is particularly useful when there is an a priori theoretical ordering of the p variables (Bock, 1975; Finn, 1974; Stevens, 1973). Roy and Bargman (1958) demonstrated that each of the successive F tests are statistically independent under the null hypothesis. The first step-down F and the univariate F ratio for that variable are identical. However, successive steps are not equivalent. The second step is the effect on the second criterion with the first criterion covaried out or removed. The third step is the effect with the first two variables' effects removed, and so on.

The appropriate technique for interpreting the step-down statistics is to begin with all p variables in the model ordered according to a priori hypotheses. The last variable is then tested with the remaining criterion variables covaried out. If this test is not significant, the next criterion variable is tested with the remaining $j-1$ (where j = number of variables still in the step-down model) variables covaried out. Testing continues in this backward selection process until a significant F for a variable is encountered. If a significant F test is found for a variable, then the variable being tested is related significantly to the classification variables over and above the $j-1$ criterion variables which are covaried out. When a significant F for a variable is encounterd, testing stops and the null hypothesis of group differences is rejected. The $j-1$ preceding variables cannot be tested separately because they are confounded with significant variation due to the jth variable. Redundancies among the variables are easily detectable with this method. It should be noted that the order of testing the variables is extremely important in this method, as the effects of the variables are considered with the preceding variables eliminated.

Some researchers might note that the step-down analysis appears similar to stepwise discriminant analysis included in many popular statistical packages. Mathematically, the two procedures can be identical (depending on the criteria for inclusion in the function); however, conceptually they are different. In general, stepwise discriminant analysis adds or deletes variables from the discriminant function based on some predetermined mathematical criteria (e.g., Wilks' lambda, Mahalanobis distance) and seeks to find the group of j variables that maximally discriminates between groups. Thus, decisions made at each step are entirely empirical. Step-down analysis requires an a priori conceptual ordering of the variables to test how a specific variable contributes to group separation given the preceding $j - 1$ variables in the function. The important difference between the techniques is whether the variables are ordered conceptually as in step-down analysis or selected empirically as in stepwise procedures (see Huberty, 1975a, 1984, for further discussion of backward and forward stepwise discriminant analysis).

Issues of Type I error must be confronted with step-down tests, since there are p significance tests that may be performed. For this reason, a Bonferroni approach is often recommended (Bock, 1975; Bock and Haggard, 1968). Increased power can be obtained for some tests by taking advantage of the fact that the overall alpha level need not be split into p equal parts; instead, the only requirement is that the p significance levels must sum to the overall level. Thus, variables that a priori are considered to contribute to group separation can be given a less stringent alpha, whereas variables that are considered to add little to group discrimination can be given more stringent alphas. Through these procedures a more parsimonious explanation of the group discrimination can be developed in which more important and perhaps simpler variables are retained instead of more dubious or complex variables.

The step-down Fs for the hypothetical data are also presented in Table 3.1. These statistics are for the model in which Y, is entered first followed by Y_2. Thus, the test of Y_2 is with the effects of Y_1 partialled out. Notice that this F test is the same as the F-to-remove and that the F test for Y_1 is the same as its univariate F. This is because it is exactly the test of Y_1 ignoring Y_2. Remember also that because the test of Y_2 is significant that testing stops at this point.

Analyzing Classification Variables

Once the multivariate null hypothesis is rejected, differences among the k groups need to be investigated. This section focuses on techniques for exploring the relationships between the k groups. The discussion of contrasts in this section assumes that (1) all p variables are tested simultaneously (i.e., a subset of the variables is not used) or (2) a contrast is coded for each variable separately (univariate contrasts). Consideration of a more general procedure in which double linear combinations of both classification and criterion variables are investigated will be discussed later.

Specific contrasts on the classification variables can be coded through dummy or contrast coding to determine how a specific group differs from another group or a linear combination of several groups

(Stevens, 1972). Depending on how the coding is performed, the contrasts may be *orthogonal*, in which the total between-groups variance is divided among $k - 1$ contrasts, or *nonorthogonal*, in which there is some overlap or correlation among the contrasts. Contrasts may also be nonorthogonal because of unequal ns in the k groups. If specific group differences are found, then use of the methods discussed in the previous section may be employed to further investigate the differences on the criterion variables. For example, inspection of the univariate F ratios or discriminant function coefficients may help clarify how the contrasting groups differ.

MULTIVARIATE CONTRASTS

If the contrasts of interest are comparisons of two groups, or more generally, any single degree of freedom contrasts, on the vector of p variables, several multivariate statistics are available to evaluate the group differences (Green, 1978; Porebski, 1966a; Stevens, 1972). The most common statistic is Hotelling's T^2. Hotelling's T^2 statistic is the multivariate generalization of the t-test, which in the more general case of $k > 2$ is equivalent to Wilks' lambda ratio when $s = \min(\gamma, p) = 1$, where γ = the degrees of freedom for the multivariate hypothesis. T^2 for two groups represents the difference between the groups on the centroids along the same direction (Porebski, 1966a). For the mathematics and a general discussion of test statistics in discriminant analysis, see Porebski (1966a).

Controlling Type I Error Rates. Just as in univariate ANOVA some steps must be taken to control the experimentwise alpha level for a set of g (where g = number of contrasts) a priori or post hoc contrasts. Very little discussion of this topic has occurred in the literature and few of the univariate post hoc procedures have been generalized to the multivariate case (Harris, 1975).

The Bonferroni technique (Bird, 1975; Miller, 1966) provides a powerful method of controlling the experimentwise error rate for any set of g contrasts. However, if the contrasts are chosen on a post hoc basis, rather than a priori, the experimentwise error rate for the Bonferroni procedure may exceed the nominal (Rodger, 1973). Thus, for any set of a priori contrasts (pairwise or other), to control the experimentwise error rate to the nominal alpha, a per comparison alpha level of α/g can be used. Harris (1975: 103-105) provides a good discussion on the use of contrasts. He suggests a set of decision rules to determine the critical F value depending on whether the linear combinations of the criterion and classification variables are a priori or post hoc.

The three multivariate pairwise contrasts for our hypothetical data indicate that Group 3 is significantly different from Group 1, F = 44.93, $p < .001$, and from Group 2, F = 39.49, $p < .001$, while Groups 1 and 2 are not significantly different from one another, F = 1.43, $p < .28$. This is also the case if one uses the more conservative Bonferroni alpha level of $.05/3 = .017$. These significant differences can be further explored on each individual variable using univariate contrasts.

UNIVARIATE CONTRASTS

If the researcher wants to investigate group differences among the p variables individually for each variable, the usual ANOVA comparison techniques (Scheffe, Tukey, etc.) are applicable. The principal choice that must be made in this case is whether to control the experimentwise error rate separately for each variable or for all p variables simultaneously. The former approach seems appropriate when Type II error is considered relatively important, because the procedure allows the experimentwise alpha for the collection of p variables to exceed the alpha level that is set by the researcher for a single variable (see Ramsey, 1980). With this approach, the first step is to perform a univariate protected F test for each variable to determine which variables display significant group differences. The second step is to search for specific group differences for those variables with significant univariate F ratios. Type I error can be controlled per variable using the usual procedures for a priori or post hoc tests (e.g., Bonferroni, Tukey, Scheffe).

A more conservative approach developed by Bird (1975) is to control alpha for either all or a subset of the contrasts and variables. Bird (1975) generalized the Bonferroni, Scheffe, and Tukey procedures to cases in which there is more than one criterion. For a set of completely a priori contrasts Bird recommends using a Bonferroni procedure in which each contrast is tested using a per comparison alpha level of α/gp. If the contrasts are partially planned and partially post hoc, then a Scheffe-Bonferroni decision rule is applied. Finally, if all of the contrasts are two group comparisons, then a Tukey-Bonferroni procedure is recommended. Bird (1975) demonstrated that these procedures can be much more powerful (the differences in power among the techniques depend on the number of groups involved) than the use of simultaneous confidence intervals, while adequately controlling the nominal alpha level. Ramsey's (1980) findings support Bird's conclusions that Bonferroni approaches are usually optimal here, because of their reasonable power and ease of application.

Analyzing Criterion
and Classification Variables
Simultaneously

The most general method of analyzing a significant MANOVA is to use Roy-Bose simultaneous confidence intervals (SCI; Morrison, 1976; Stevens, 1973). This is a completely multivariate approach in which any linear combination of the classification or criterion variables can be investigated. In this manner double linear combinations of classification and criterion variables can be formed. The experimentwise alpha is controlled to the nominal alpha for any number of contrasts among the k groups and p variables. The extreme generality of the method is also one of the major drawbacks. Hummel and Sligo (1971) demonstrated in a Monte Carlo study that use of SCIs is an extremely conservative method. In fact, the conservativeness increases as N, p, and the proportion of variance in common among the p variables increase. For this reason Stevens (1973) recommends using a more liberal alpha level of .10 to increase the power of the test. Mathematically the technique is ideal because of its generality; however, in practical applications it is often not very useful.

The Roy-Bose SCI is based on Roy's greatest characteristic root (GCR) test statistic described in Section 2 for the overall MANOVA test. As Bird and Hadzi-Pavlovic (1983) point out, there are other simultaneous test procedures (STPs) based on the other overall MANOVA test statistics (e.g., the Pillai-Bartlett trace, Wilks' lambda). Because the Pillai-Bartlett V test statistic has certain advantages for the overall MANOVA test (see the earlier discussion in Section 2), it might seem that follow-up tests should also be based on the Pillai-Bartlett trace. However, Bird and Hadzi-Pavlovic (1983) present Monte Carlo data showing that the STP based on V can be extremely conservative compared to the STP based on Roy's GCR. Their data also show that the Roy-Bose approach tends to be relatively robust to violations of assumptions as long as tests are restricted to interpretable contrasts on linear combinations of variables of theoretical interest as opposed to data-determined contrasts.

An example of the above simultaneous test procedure recommended by Bird and Hadzi-Pavlovic (1983) is illustrated by a comparison conducted on the hypothetical data. Recall from Section 2 that group differences were maximized on V_1, which was found to be $-.55Y_1$ + $.42Y_2$. Group means on V_1 were 19.5, 19.1, and 13.3 for groups 1, 2, and 3, respectively. To facilitate interpretation, we might want to test whether the average of groups 1 and 2 differ from group 3 on the unweighted difference between Y_1 and Y_2. To test this double contrast we would need the following information: SS(contrast)/SS(contrast) + SS(within) for this new transformed variable. For these data this equals: $480/(480 + 54) = 0.899$. To find the critical value we could use Harris's (1975) table of Roy's GCR. We need to know the values of $s = 2$, $m = -.5$, and $n = 4.5$, which implies a critical value for alpha = .05 of 0.533 (using interpolation of the tabled values). As the observed value is greater than the critical value, we reject the null hypothesis.

Numerical Example

We will continue with the Fletcher and Satz example from Section 2 to further demonstrate with real data the use of the techniques discussed in this section. Recall that the omnibus test was significant. Also remember that there are s possible roots that can be significant for the multivariate test. The Wilks' lambda criterion indicates that there is a second significant discriminant function, multivariate $F(10, 1125) = 2.49$, $p < .006$ (see Dimension Reduction Analysis, Table 3.2). In contrast, when the characteristic roots are tested individually using the GCR criterion, the second root barely misses significance at the .05 level. This discrepancy between the likelihood ratio approach and the GCR approach is not entirely surprising, as pointed out by Harris (1975, 1976). We will further illustrate the use of the various analytic methods for both roots to interpret the overall differences.

The univariate F tests (see Table 3.2) for each criterion are statistically significant. The standardized discriminant weights (SDW) indicate that the variables EF, VF, and SIM are most important for group separation on Function 1. On Function 2 the PPVT has the largest SDW with RD, EF, and VF contributing highly as well. Inspection of the canonical variate correlations (CVC) indicates that all the dependent variables correlate highly with Function 1, with the tests EF and SIM having the highest correlations. The PPVT has the highest correlation with Function 2, followed by RD, EF, and VF. VMI and SIM correlate very little with Function 2. The F-to-remove statistics indicate that the variables SIM, EF, and VF are most important for group separation, while the variable RD is least important for group separation. Also

TABLE 3.2
Analyses and Statistics for Fletcher and Satz
Real Data Numerical Example

	Dimension Reduction Analysis				
Function	Wilks' lambda	Approx. F	Hyp df	Err df	p <
1 to 3	.59626	17.72	18	1590.06	.001
2 to 3	.95721	2.49	10	1125.00	.006
3 to 3	.99777	0.32	4	563.00	.868

	Variable					
Statistic	PPVT	RD	EF	VF	VMI	SIM
Univariate F (3,567)	26.85	31.43	61.25	32.74	29.31	47.47
F-to-remove (3,567)	6.49	1.86	8.61	8.38	5.66	13.37
SDW						
Function 1	.15	.10	.39	.33	.29	.44
Function 2	.95	−.51	−.58	.37	.12	−.02
CVC						
Function 1	.46	.52	.73	.53	.50	.64
Function 2	.52	−.37	−.36	.33	−.10	.04

NOTE: SDW = standardized discriminant weight; CVC = canonical variate correlation.

notice how these statistics differ from the univariate F tests. This is because the correlations among the variables are considered in the F-to-remove statistics.

Figure 3.1 presents a plot of the group centroids in two dimensional discriminant space. The plot of the centroids illustrates that the first discriminant function primarily separates each of the groups, while the second discriminant function primarily separates the superior readers from the other three groups. The measurement vectors for the original variables are also displayed in Figure 3.1 (see Overall and Klett, 1972). The vectors originate from the grand mean of the group centroids. The direction of the vectors indicates as expected that the superior readers scored highest and the severely disabled readers scored lowest on all six criteria. Recall that the length of each vector is proportional to the univariate F value for that variable. The vectors reveal the additional information that the PPVT mostly discriminates the superior readers from the other three groups, whereas the EF tends to discriminate among all the groups, especially the severely disabled from the others.

If only the univariate Fs are used to interpret the data, all the dependent variables appear important for determining differences between the groups. However, only by using the discriminant analysis is it clear that there are two underlying dimensions. Using both the SDWs and the CVCs, it appears that the first dimension represents differences on higher-order verbal and nonverbal abilities, whereas the second dimension is primarily an overall verbal intelligence dimension.

It should be noted that there are differences between the pattern of results for the univariate Fs, Fs-to-remove, SDWs, and CVCs. This is due to the different questions answered by the various approaches. The univariate Fs indicate the magnitude of group differences on each variable individually without consideration of the other variables. The SDWs reflect the unique contribution of each variable in the context of the other variates for a specific discriminant function, whereas the F-to-remove index indicates the unique contribution of each variable considering the other variables across *all* of the dimensions. The CVCs measure the correlation of each variate with scores on each discriminant function. Given the intercorrelations among these variables, it is not surprising that the unique contribution of a variable (i.e., the SDW) tends to be less than the corresponding CVC.

With more than two groups, just as in a univariate ANOVA, the next step in the analysis is to determine which groups are responsible for the significant difference obtained in the overall test. The remaining examples analyze one possible contrast chosen for purposes of demonstration.

A pairwise contrast between the superior and severely disabled readers indicates that the groups are significantly different, multivariate $F(6, 562) = 51.84, p < .001$. If all six pairwise contrasts among the four groups are carried out, the appropriate alpha level is $\alpha/g = .05/6 = .008$ for each contrast. If further contrasts on all the univariate variables are conducted, the appropriate alpha for each of these comparisons is $\alpha/gp = .05/(6 \times 6) = .0014$ (Bird, 1975).

Other contrasts could be conducted in a similar manner to further understand the differences between the groups. The type of analyses performed would depend on the research questions to be answered and the nature of the differences found in the data. We will further exemplify these techniques in the next section.

4. CAUSAL MODELS
UNDERLYING MANOVA ANALYSES

Purpose of Path-Analytic Representations

Path-analytic representations are developed in this section for the various techniques used in MANOVA analyses. Recognition of the causal models implicitly underlying the various methods clarifies the relationships among the strategies. The primary purpose of this section is pedagogical, in that the path diagrams to be presented for different methods often enhance understanding of the questions addressed by these methods. However, it is generally preferable to perform the actual data analysis using MANOVA computational formulas such as those presented in Section 2, rather than directly through a path-analytic representation. Bagozzi et al. (1981) provide details on how to obtain MANOVA results from the path-analytic approach using LISREL (Joreskog and Sorbom, 1983). Our purpose here, however, is primarily conceptual.

Several authors (Bentler and Huba, 1982; Blalock, 1969; Dwyer, 1983; Kenny, 1979; Van de Geer, 1971) have used path analysis to relate different multivariate techniques such as factor analysis, discriminant analysis, regression analysis, and canonical correlation analysis. Kenny (1979: 203-205) discusses several models for analysis of variance with more than one dependent measure. We will discuss such models in the context of alternative strategies to follow-up a significant omnibus MANOVA test. However, at the outset it should be emphasized that causal inferences are possible when using causal models only if a set of restrictive assumptions is satisfied (see Kenny, 1979: 51). In particular, conceptualizing MANOVA in path-analytic terms has no effect on the appropriateness of making a causal inference concerning group differences.

Overview of Path-Analytic
Representation of MANOVA

We will introduce the basic ideas of path analysis in the specific context of the overall MANOVA test. Readers interested in more general introductions to path analysis should consult such references as Asher (1976), Bentler (1980), Duncan (1975), Dwyer (1983), or Kenny (1979). Figure 4.1 presents a path diagram for a two-group, three-

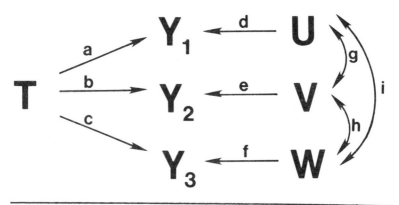

Figure 4.1

variable design. Each of the 7 capital letters in the diagram represents a variable thought to be either a cause or an effect in the system.

For example, T is a dummy variable that represents group membership; such a variable is typically coded 0 for subjects in one group and 1 for subjects in the other group. Y_1, Y_2, and Y_3 represent the three dependent variables. The letters U, V, and W represent disturbance terms (i.e., error terms). In general, disturbance terms represent sources of influence on the dependent variables not otherwise accounted for in the diagram. In the case of our diagram, then, U represents all causes of Y_1 other than T (that is, other than group membership). You may recall from Section 2 that this is precisely the meaning of "error" in analysis of variance models. The 6 single-sided arrows represent causal effects from one variable to another. Thus, for example, the diagram stipulates that Y is caused by T and U. The disturbances are connected to each other by two-sided arrows because they are assumed to be correlated, but without a specification of which disturbance is a cause and which is an effect of the others. An arrow, whether one-sided or two-sided, is often referred to as a "path," leading to the name "path diagram" for the picture as a whole. The lower-case letter associated with each path is called a path coefficient (or, more generally, a structural coefficient) and represents the strength of that path. It can be shown that in this model the path coefficients a, b, and c equal the correlations of T with Y_1, Y_2, and Y_3, respectively. (Readers interested in further details are referred to Kenny's [1979] discussion of the "tracing rule".)

A primary purpose of path analysis is typically to compare different models for a given set of data. For example, a researcher might believe that the two groups represented by the dummy variable in Figure 4.1 do not differ on the Y_1 variable. In this case, T and Y_1 would be uncorrelated, so that a = 0, implying that the path from T to Y_1 is unnecessary. Whether such a parsimonious model provided an adequate explanation of a set of data could be tested by performing a significance test of the correlation between T and Y_1. In general, it is possible to test the adequacy of parsimonious models with one or more omitted paths, because such models imply that certain correlational patterns should occur. We will now consider this idea in more detail for the specific model depicted in Figure 4.1.

Omnibus MANOVA Test

The omnibus MANOVA null hypothesis states that all groups have the same population means on all dependent variables. In terms of Figure 4.1, the null hypothesis states that the dummy variable T correlates zero with Y_1, Y_2, and Y_3 in the population. As previously stated, these three correlations equal the population values of the a, b, and c path coefficients, respectively. Thus, in terms of the path diagram, the omnibus MANOVA null hypothesis is that a, b, and c all equal zero, in which case the paths from T to Y_1, Y_2, and Y_3 can be omitted. In other words, the overall MANOVA test can be conceptualized as a comparison of the model depicted in Figure 4.1 versus an alternate model in which the paths from T to Y_1, Y_2, and Y_3 have all been omitted. In the terminology of Section 2, the model shown in Figure 4.1 is the "full" model, whereas the alternate model, in which the a, b, and c paths are omitted, is the "reduced" model.

Univariate Tests

Suppose the overall MANOVA null hypothesis is rejected. As discussed in Section 3, one follow-up procedure is to conduct univariate F tests. The path diagram depicted in Figure 4.1 can also be used to conceptualize univariate tests. Whereas the multivariate test considered a, b, and c simultaneously, the univariate approach considers each coefficient separately. The test of statistical significance for each coefficient individually is simply a test that the correlation between the dummy variable and the particular dependent variable is zero. However, this test is equivalent to the t-test of group mean differences on the

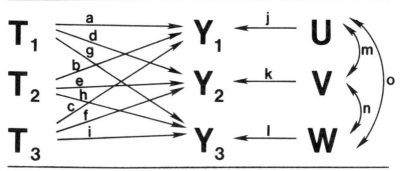

Figure 4.2

dependent variable. This path-analytic representation shows clearly that the univariate follow-up tests represent an attempt to achieve a parsimonious model by omitting unnecessary paths. We will see later that the other follow-up procedures also strive for parsimony, but consider different ways of omitting paths.

Figure 4.2 shows a path model for a more complex study involving four treatment groups and three criterion variables. For simplicity, it is assumed that orthogonal coding has been used to represent group membership ("orthogonality" simply means that no arrows between the three T variables are needed), although this is not necessary. It can easily be shown that the principles developed for the simpler model in Figure 4.1 also hold for the model in Figure 4.2. For example, the omnibus MANOVA test hypothesizes that the 9 path coefficients a through i are all equal to zero. Similarly, a simultaneous test of the a, b, and c coefficients in Figure 4.2 is equivalent to the univariate F test for Y_1.

In the general case of k groups and p dependent variables, there are $k - 1$ dummy variables. Each of these variables may have a path to each dependent variable, implying a total of $p (k - 1)$ possible paths. The multivariate null hypothesis is false if and only if at least one of the $p (k - 1)$ paths is nonzero in the population. Notice that this explains why the tests of significance for Wilks' lambda and the Pillai-Bartlett trace have $p (k - 1)$ numerator degrees of freedom in the F distribution. The goal of the univariate F follow-up approach is to achieve parsimony by examining p collections of $k - 1$ paths to discover which sets of $k - 1$ paths are nonzero and, hence, need to be retained in the model. It should be noted that analysis of classification variables is often the next step,

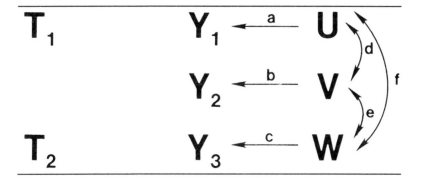

Figure 4.3

whereby individual paths in the different sets of k - I paths are tested for significance.

Discriminant Analysis Model

The model for discriminant analysis is very different from the path model for individual univariate tests. To consider the discriminant analysis approach, it is necessary to consider a sequence of several path diagrams. Figures 4.3, 4.4, and 4.5 illustrate models for a 3-group, 3-variable design, where T_1 and T_2 are dummy variables that represent group membership (orthogonal coding is again assumed for simplicity), the Ys represent the dependent variables, and U, V, and W are disturbance terms. Three groups are used here, because with only two groups there can be only one discriminant function by mathematical necessity.

These models include a new type of variable, represented by y (Figures 4.4 and 4.5) and y* (Figure 4.5), which are unobserved variables. These unobserved variables can be conceptualized as latent variables that are assumed to be exact linear functions of the T variables. In this type of model, called a MIMIC model (Joreskog and Goldberger, 1975), there are no disturbance terms associated with y and y* because there are no unknown causes of these variables.

The models represented in Figures 4.3, 4.4, and 4.5 differ in the number of factors hypothesized to exist. Discriminant analysis significance tests can best be understood by comparing the three models. The model that assumes no underlying factors (Figure 4.3) allows no population correlation between the T variables and Y_1, Y_2, and Y_3. This zero

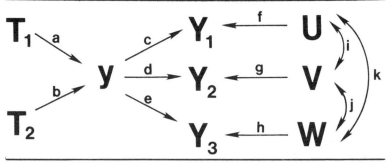

Figure 4.4

correlation implies that the largest population canonical correlation between the T set and the Y set is zero. This is the hypothesis tested by the greatest characteristic root approach (Harris, 1975; Morrison, 1976). Of course, if the largest canonical R is zero, so are the remaining $s - 1$ values. In contrast, the other 3 overall MANOVA test statistics test the hypothesis that all s values are simultaneously zero. Although both approaches test the overall multivariate null hypothesis, a significant result with the Pillai-Bartlett, Wilks' lambda, or Hotelling-Lawley approaches implies that one of the $p(k - 1)$ paths of Figure 4.1 is nonzero, whereas a significant GCR result implies that at least one factor is necessary to explain the relationship of the T variables to the criterion measures. If the GCR test yields a significant result, the model of Figure 4.3 is insufficient. In this case, a model at least as complex as that in Figure 4.4 is required, because at least one factor is necessary. Discriminant analysis then proceeds to test whether another factor is necessary to explain treatment effects; that is, whether a second discriminant function discriminates between the groups. Hauser and Goldberger (1971) and Kenny (1979) demonstrate that if the model represented in Figure 4.4 is correct, the second largest population canonical correlation is zero. The null hypothesis that this canonical R is zero can be tested by examining the second largest characteristic root of the appropriate matrix (see Harris, 1975: 108, 134). If the second largest population canonical R is zero, then so are the remaining $s - 2$ values. Many authors (Cooley and Lohnes, 1971; Overall and Klett, 1972; Tatsuoka, 1971) recommend a simultaneous test of roots 2 through s rather than simply a test of the second root. Harris (1975, 1976) argues that the use of such a procedure, called partitioned-U tests, is invalid for

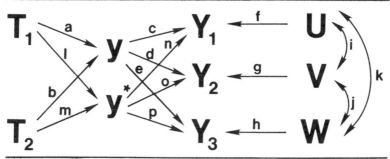

Figure 4.5

several reasons. The reader is referred to Harris (1976), Mendoza et al. (1978), and Chou and Muirhead (1979) for further discussion of this controversy.

The models in Figures 4.3, 4.4, and 4.5 illustrate how discriminant analysis determines the number of factors needed to relate treatment effects to criterion measures. Obviously, if Figure 4.3 represents the correct model, no factors are needed, because there are no treatment effects. With a single factor, as depicted in Figure 4.4, there is homogeneity of the T variables with the Y variables. The geometric meaning of homogeneity is that a single dimension (the linear discriminant function) is sufficient to explain group differences. Examination of the path coefficients of Figure 4.4 indicates that the algebraic equivalent of the geometric statement is that the correlation between any treatment dummy variable and any dependent measure equals the product of the two corresponding paths. This implies that the treatment effect can be accounted for by assuming that the p criterion measures are indicators of a single construct. The p measures differ only in the amount by which they are affected, as represented by path coefficients for the measures.

Comparison of Figures 4.3, 4.4, and 4.5 with the diagrams for the univariate approach (Figures 4.1 and 4.2) illustrates how the two strategies differ. Both techniques strive to achieve parsimony by reducing the number of path coefficients needed in the diagram, but they do so in very different ways.

Model for the Step-Down Tests

The use of step-down tests can also be represented by a path analysis diagram. Figure 4.6 is such a diagram for a 2-group, 3-variable design,

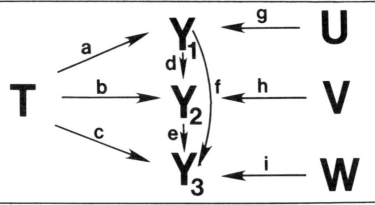

Figure 4.6

where T is again a dummy variable for group membership, the Ys represent the dependent variables, and U, V, and W are disturbance terms. This path diagram corresponds to the following set of structural equations:

$$Y_1 = aT + gU$$

$$Y_2 = dY_1 + bT + hV$$

$$Y_3 = fY_1 + eY_2 + cT + iW$$

This set of equations is a recursive set; therefore, estimates of the path coefficients and significance tests can be performed with ordinary least squares. Specifically, the Y on the left-hand side of an equation is regressed on the variables on the right-hand side of the equation. Thus Y_1 is regressed on T, while Y_2 is regressed on Y_1 and T, and Y_3 is regressed on Y_1, Y_2, and T. The significance test of T in each case corresponds to an ANCOVA test, in which all prior Y variables are included as covariates. However, as previously discussed, this is precisely the way in which step-down tests are conducted.

The meaning of the step-down approach can best be understood by contrasting Figure 4.6 with the figures for the univariate approach (Figures 4.1 and 4.2) and the discriminant analysis approach (Figures 4.3, 4.4, and 4.5). Comparison of the six diagrams shows that the step-down approach is unique in assuming a causal ordering rather than

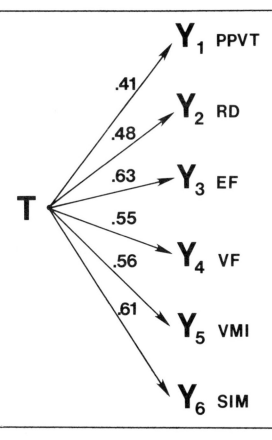

Figure 4.7

simply a correlation among the criterion variables. With this approach, it is possible to separate direct and indirect effects of the treatment on each dependent variable.

Extension of these models to the remaining techniques is straightforward. Investigation of the classification variables is accomplished by coding the T variables to represent specific contrasts. Simultaneous tests of various paths are conducted depending on whether the researcher is interested in univariate or multivariate comparisons. However, many of the issues in analyzing the classification variables (e.g., experimentwise error rate) do not affect the underlying structural model.

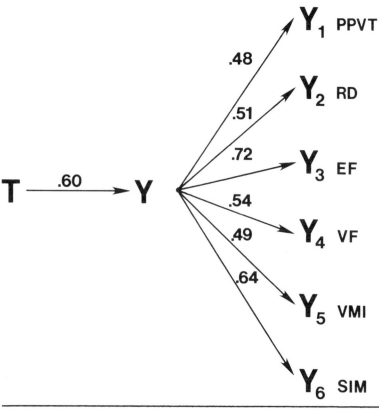

Figure 4.8

MANOVA and LISREL

Readers who are familiar with LISREL may realize that LISREL can be used to analyze group differences in factor means (Sorbom, 1974). It should be emphasized that testing for differences in factor means answers a different question than MANOVA addresses, even if a path-analytic representation of MANOVA is considered. The ways in which LISREL and MANOVA differ can be considered at a conceptual level by referring back to Figure 4.4. Recall that in the discriminant analysis model there is no disturbance for *y*, and the *U*, *V*, and *W* disturbance terms are allowed to correlate. In the LISREL approach there would be a disturbance term associated with *y*, because *y* would be conceptualized

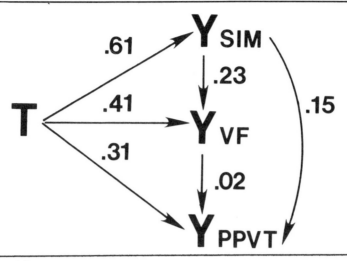

Figure 4.9

as a latent variable with multiple causes in addition to T_1 and T_2. Also, the latent variable y would be viewed as the sole common cause of Y_1, Y_2, and Y_3, so that the U, V, and W disturbance terms would not be allowed to correlate with one another. As a consequence of these changes from the discriminant analysis model, the LISREL test of factor means addresses a hypothesis that is different from the MANOVA hypothesis. Specifically, in the LISREL test of factor means the model stipulates that those observed variables with the largest factor loadings should display the largest group differences, because the underlying factor is the sole common cause of the Ys. For further details, the reader is referred to Sorbom (1974).

Numerical Example

Figures 4.7, 4.8, and 4.9 present the contrast between superior and severely disabled readers in the Fletcher and Satz (1980) study from the perspective of causal models. T is a dummy variable coded 0 for severely disabled readers and coded 1 for superior readers. In all cases, disturbance terms as well as any correlations among the disturbances have been omitted from the figures for simplicity.

Figure 4.7 presents the diagram corresponding to the overall MANOVA test (see Figure 4.1). The positive values of the paths from T

to each Y variable indicate that the superior readers score higher on the average than the severely disabled readers on all six variables. All six paths are needed, because the overall MANOVA test and all six univariate tests are statistically significant.

Figure 4.8 presents the path representation for a discriminant analysis model with one factor (the maximum number for contrasting two groups). The path from T to Y is needed because there is a significant correlation between the dummy variable and discriminant variate. The paths from Y to each variable represent the respective CVCs. The figure shows that EF and SIM correlate most highly with the discriminant variate.

It might be expected that the group differences on specific verbal skills tests SIM and VF would subsume any differences on the general verbal IQ measure, PPVT. Figure 4.9 displays this step-down model for these data. The paths from T to PPVT and VF are both relatively large (0.31 and 0.41, respectively), and are statistically significant at the .05 level. They are also significant at the .025 level, if a Bonferroni adjustment is applied (Bock, 1975). Thus, group differences on the PPVT cannot be explained simply in terms of SIM and VF.

5. COMPLEX DESIGNS

In this section we will briefly discuss the use of MANOVA techniques in more complex research designs. Factorial MANOVAs, repeated measure designs, profile analysis, and multivariate analysis of covariance will be reviewed. Special issues for each of these topics will be discussed.

Higher-Order MANOVA

The extension of the techniques covered thus far to factorial design MANOVAs is generally straightforward. As with factorial designs in ANOVA, each main effect and interaction is tested separately. If the multivariate test of interaction is significant, multivariate tests of simple effects are typically conducted. In MANOVA this consists of performing a separate multivariate test for each effect. If a given effect is significant, it is further analyzed and interpreted using the techniques described in Section 3. If a specific effect is not significant, no further analyses are conducted.

For example, in a 3-way factorial design the first step is to test the 3-way interaction, then test the 3 2-way interactions, and finally test the 3 main effects. If any of the interactions are significant, the remaining lower-order effects are usually analyzed and interpreted in the context of the interactive effects of the factors (Kirk, 1982).

If all cells have equal sample sizes, the effects are orthogonal and can be tested individually. However, if the cell sizes are unequal, then the effects are nonorthogonal and the correlations between the effects must be considered in the analysis. See Appelbaum and Cramer (1974) for further discussion of these issues.

Repeated Measures Designs

In repeated measures designs or *within-subject designs,* multiple measures on each subject for different trials or times are collected using the same criterion variable at each trial or time. These criteria can be viewed as separate variables statistically and tested using MANOVA. A primary advantage of this design is that it controls for individual differences and often produces a more powerful test of the hypothesis than would a between-subject design. The traditional way to analyze this type of data is to use a mixed-model ANOVA (McCall and Appelbaum, 1973). However, there is a restrictive assumption that must be met or the mixed-model test will have an inflated alpha level (see Harris, 1975; Kirk, 1982; McCall and Appelbaum, 1973, for a discussion of these issues). The major assumption required by the mixed-model approach is that the variance-covariance matrix exhibit sphericity (Kirk, 1982), which most matrices resulting from social sciences data do not exhibit. This assumption is not required by the multivariate approach to repeated measures. In factorial designs there may be multiple within-subject factors and/or between-subject factors. Again, each effect is tested separately and further analyses are used to interpret the differences.

Profile Analysis

When a design consists of one or more between-subject factors and a within-subject factor, an alternate name sometimes given to the analysis is profile analysis (Morrison, 1976). The within-subject factor might be time, different scales on a test, or scores on a criterion measure under different conditions. In order for a profile analysis to be meaningful, the levels of the within-subject factor (i.e., the response variables) should be "commensurate," which means that they are measured in comparable units. When this condition is not met, the response variables should be thought of as conceptually distinct and a between-subject MANOVA should be performed on the set of dependent variables.

If the design is conceptualized as a 2-factor design, with one within-subject and one between-subject factor, 3 tests can be performed. The same 3 tests are conducted in a profile analysis. First is the test of the parallelism hypothesis, which asks whether the group profiles show the same pattern or shape across the different variables. This is equivalent to the test of the interaction between the classification and criterion variables. This question can be answered by forming $p - 1$ new variables (represented here by W), each of which represents the difference between two "adjacent" dependent variables, $W_i = Y_i - Y_{i+1}$. Parallelism is tested by performing a MANOVA on these $p - 1$ new variables. Notice that a significant result here implies that the difference between the variables are not the same for all groups, which in turn implies that the group profiles are not parallel.

The second test is of the levels hypothesis, which asks whether the profiles for the group means are at the same level. This is a univariate test, in which the dependent variable is the average of the p variables for each subject.

The third test is of the flatness hypothesis, which asks whether the "pooled" profile, ignoring group differences, is flat. In other words, this tests whether the p grand means (averaging over groups) on the criterion variables are identical to one another. If the parallelism hypothesis is rejected, then the other tests must be interpreted in light of the interaction between the within and between factors. Again, it should be noted that in order to perform a profile analysis, the criterion variables must all be on the same scale and must provide some meaningful conception of the subjects.

Doubly Multivariate Designs

An additional complexity that sometimes arises in repeated measures designs is that more than one qualitatively distinct variable is measured on more than one occasion. This type of design is often referred to as "doubly multivariate," because it is multivariate for two reasons. First, there are two or more conceptually distinct dependent variables. Second, each variable is measured more than once in a repeated measures fashion. Bock (1975: 502-505) discusses the analysis for this design.

It might be helpful at this point to give an example of an actual study that employed this design. Albright et al. (1984) were interested in comparing the physiological reactions of Type A and Type B coronary-prone behavior type individuals in stresssful situations. Their design consisted of two between-subject factors (behavior type and level of stress induced by the experimentor) and one within-subject factor (time). Two dependent measures (systolic blood pressure and heart rate) were obtained for each subject at each time, leading to a doubly multi-variate design. A number of statistically significant results were obtained, the most interesting of which was a multivariate main effect for behavior type. Follow-up univariate tests failed to produce significance at the .05 level for either blood pressure or heart rate. As discussed in Sections 2 and 3, such a result is entirely possible, because there are situations in which the multivariate test is more powerful than the univariate tests.

Multivariate Analysis of Covariance

If one or more variables are collected to statistically control for sources of variation with multiple criterion variables, then multivariate analysis of covariance (MANCOVA) is the appropriate method of analysis. Although MANCOVA is a simple conceptual extension of ANCOVA, mathematically and practically it is much more complicated. In addition, there has been relatively little work investigating its use and properties.

Probably the most common design in which MANCOVA would be used is in a multiple-group pretest-posttest design, in which a set of variables has been measured both at the posttest and at the pretest. The reader is referred to Barcikowski (1983), Bock (1975), or Timm (1975) for further details of MANCOVA.

6. OVERVIEW OF COMPUTER PROGRAMS FOR MANOVA

Most of the overall and follow-up procedures we have described can be performed rather easily on a computer with widely available statistical packages. The purpose of this section is to provide a brief overview of capabilities of MANOVA programs. A caveat must be offered at the

TABLE 6.1
Capabilities of BMDP, SAS, and SPSS-X MANOVA Programs

Capability	BMDP P4V	BMDP P7M	SAS GLM	SAS ANOVA	SAS CANDISC	SPSS-X MANOVA
I. Omnibus Tests						
4 test statistics	✓		✓a	✓a	✓	✓a
automatic processing of balanced (equal n) factorial design	✓		✓	✓		✓
unbalanced factorial design	✓		✓			✓
automatic processing of repeated measures designs	✓					✓
inspection of multivariate outliers	✓		✓			✓
eigenvalues of HE^{-1} matrix						✓
canonical correlations	✓	✓	✓	✓	✓	✓
II. Analysis of Criterion Variables						
univariate F tests	✓f	✓b	✓		✓	✓
standardized discriminant weights	✓f	✓f			✓	✓
rotated discriminant weights						✓
canonical structure correlations		✓			✓	✓
number of significant functions					✓c	✓c
plot of group centroids		✓				
insert measurement vectors						
step-down tests	✓d	✓	✓d		✓g	✓h
F-to-remove	✓	✓				✓
III. Analysis of Classification Variables						
multivariate contrasts	✓	✓	✓			✓
univariate contrasts	✓	✓	✓	✓e		✓
IV. Analysis of Criterion and Classification Variables						
simultaneous confidence intervals						

NOTE: a = no p-value for GCR test; b = no p-values; c = partitioned-U test; d = requires successive ANCOVAs; e = pairwise comparisons only; f = raw coefficients only; g = available in PROC STEPDISC of SAS; h = available in SPSS-X DISCRIMINANT.

beginning, because major distributors of software packages constantly add enhancements to their programs. Thus, specific comparisons among programs may become dated rapidly. Nevertheless, it may be informative to consider the software options available for MANOVA as of this writing.

Although several special-purpose MANOVA packages are available, our review will cover only those MANOVA procedures available in BMDP, SAS, and SPSS-X, because these are the three most widely used statistical packages. Each of these packages has at least two procedures for performing MANOVA analyses. Table 6.1 shows some of the capabilities of two BMDP programs, three SAS programs, and one SPSS-X program. In addition to the general caveat mentioned above about changes in programs, we should also state that the capabilities in Table 6.1 are by no means the sole criteria for evaluating MANOVA software. Some obvious additional criteria are ease of use, quality and quantity of documentation, and accuracy of computational algorithms. Our much more limited purpose in Table 6.1 is simply to indicate whether specific techniques we have discussed are available in each of the programs. It should also be noted that other programs performing some special cases of MANOVA are BMDP3D in BMDP, STEPDISC in SAS, and DISCRIMINANT in SPSS-X. Also, additional comparisons of analysis of variance programs appear in Hosking and Hamer (1979) and Tabachnick and Fidell (1983). One other useful reference is Barcikowski (1983), which is a 3-volume collection of annotated input and output of analysis of variance programs. One volume is devoted to BMDP, a second to SAS, and a third to SPSS-X.

Finally, programs have recently become available for performing MANOVA analyses on microcomputers. Although the list of available programs is certain to grow, two programs available as of this writing that are quite impressive are GANOVA and SYSTAT. GANOVA is described in the February 1984 issue of *The American Statistician*. SYSTAT is one of 24 microcomputer statistical packages reviewed in the April 1984 issue of *BYTE* magazine. Further information on these programs is available from the authors of these reviews, whose addresses are given in the aforementioned publications. Also of significance is that BMDP recently announced that its entire set of programs will be available for the IBM personal computer and compatibles.

REFERENCES

ALBRIGHT, C., R. I. EVANS, S. E. MAXWELL, and R. DEMBROSKI (1984) "Relationship between Type A coronary prone behavior and physiological reactivity during an anxiety-provoking verbal task." (unpublished manuscript)

ANDERSON, T. W. (1958) An Introduction to Multivariate Statistical Analysis. New York: John Wiley.

APPELBAUM, M. I. and E. M. CRAMER (1974) "Some problems in the nonorthogonal analysis of variance." Psychological Bulletin 81: 335-343.

ASHER, H. B. (1976) Causal Modeling. Beverly Hills, CA: Sage.

BAGOZZI, R. P., C. FORNELL, and D. F. LARCKER (1981) "Canonical correlation analysis as a special case of a structural relations model." Multivariate Behavioral Research 16: 437-454.

BARCIKOWSKI, R. S. [ed.] (1983) Computer Packages and Research Design with Annotations of Input and Output from the BMDP, SAS, SPSS, and SPSSX Statistical Packages. Washington, DC: University Press of America.

———and J. P. STEVENS (1975) "A Monte Carlo study of the stability of canonical correlations, canonical weights, and canonical variate variable correlations." Multivariate Behavioral Research 10: 353-364.

BARGMAN, R. E. (1970) "Interpretation and use of a generalized discriminant function," in R. C. Bose et al. (eds.) Essays in Probability and Statistics. Chapel Hill: University of North Carolina Press.

BARTLETT, M. S. (1947) "Multivariate analysis." Journal of the Royal Statistical Society Supplement, Series B 9: 176-197.

BENTLER, P. M. (1980) "Multivariate analysis with latent variables: causal modeling." Annual Review of Psychology 31: 419-456.

BIRD, K. D. (1975) "Simultaneous contrast testing procedures for multivariate experiments." Multivariate Behavioral Research 10: 343-351.

———and D. HADZI-PAVLOVIC (1983) "Simultaneous test procedures and the choice of a test statistic in MANOVA." Psychological Bulletin 93: 167-178.

BLALOCK, H. M. (1969) Theory Construction. Englewood Cliffs, NJ: Prentice-Hall.

BOCK, R. D. (1975) Multivariate Statistical Methods in Behavioral Research. New York: McGraw-Hill.

———and E. A. HAGGARD (1968) "The use of multivariate analysis of variance in behavioral research," in D. Whitla (ed.) Handbook of Measurement and Assessment Sciences. Reading, MA: Addison-Wesley.

BORGAN, F. H. and M. J. SELIG (1978) "Uses of discriminate analysis following MANOVA: multivariate statistics for multivariate purposes." Journal of Applied Psychology 63: 689-697.

BRAY, J. H. and S. E. MAXWELL (1982) "Analyzing and interpreting significant MANOVAs." Review of Educational Research 52: 340-367.

CARROLL, J. B. (1961) "The nature of the data, or how to choose a correlation coefficient." Psychometrika 26: 347-372.

CHOU, K. J. and R. J. MUIRHEAD (1979) "On some distribution problems in MANOVA and discriminant analysis." Journal of Multivariate Analysis 9: 410-419.

COLE, D. A., G. S. HOWARD, and S. E. MAXWELL (1981) "Effects of mono- versus multiple-operationalization in construct validation efforts." Journal of Consulting and Clinical Psychology 49: 395.

COOLEY, W. W. and P. R. LOHNES (1971) Multivariate Data Analysis. New York: John Wiley.

CRAMER, E. M. and R. D. BOCK (1966) "Multivariate analysis." Review of Educational Research 36: 604-617.

CRAMER, E. M. and W. A. NICEWANDER (1979) "Some symmetric, invariant measures of multivariate association." Psychometrika 44: 43-54.

DARLINGTON, R. B. (1968) "Multiple regression in psychological research and practice." Psychological Bulletin 69: 161-182.

———S. L. WEINBERG, and H. J. WALBERG (1973) "Canonical variate analysis and related techniques." Review of Educational Research 43: 443-454.

DUNCAN, O. D. (1975) Introduction to Structural Equation Models. New York: Academic.

DWYER, J. H. (1983) Statistical Models for the Social and Behavioral Sciences. New York: Oxford University Press.

EVERITT, B. S. (1978) Graphical Techniques for Multivariate Data. London: Heineman Educational Books.

FINN, J. D. (1974) A General Model for Multivariate Analysis. New York: Holt, Rinehart & Winston.

FLETCHER, J. M., W. J. RICE, and R. M. RAY (1978) "Linear discriminant function analysis in neuropsychological research: some uses and abuses." Cortex 14: 564-577.

GABRIEL, R. M. (1979) "Post-MANOVA data analysis: six alternatives and criteria for selection." Presented at the American Psychological Association, New York.

GNANADESIKAN, R. (1977) Methods for Statistical Data of Multivariate Observations. New York: John Wiley.

GREEN, P. E. (1978) Analyzing Multivariate Data. Hinsdale, IL: Dryden Press.

———and J. D. CARROLL (1976) Mathematical Tools for Applied Multivariate Analysis. New York: Academic.

HAKSTIAN, A. R., J. C. ROED, and J. C. LIND (1979) "Two-sample T2 procedure and the assumption of homogeneous covariance matrices." Psychological Bulletin 86: 1255-1263.

HARRIS, R. J. (1976) "The invalidity of partitioned-U tests in canonical correlation and multivariate analysis of variance." Multivariate Behavioral Research 11: 353-365.

———(1975) A Primer of Multivariate Statistics. New York: Academic.

HAUSER, R. M. and A. S. GOLDBERGER (1977) "The treatment of unobservable variables in path analysis," in H. L. Costner (ed.) Sociological Methodology, 1977. San Francisco: Jossey-Bass.

HOSKING, J. D. and R. M. HAMER (1979) "Nonorthogonal analysis of variance programs: an evaluation." Journal of Educational Statistics 4: 161-188.

HUBERTY, C. J. (1984) "Issues in the use and interpretation of discriminant analysis." Psychological Bulletin 95: 156-171.
———(1976) "The stability of three indices of variable contribution in discriminant analysis." Journal of Experimental Education 45.
———(1975) "Discriminant analysis." Review of Educational Research 45: 543-598.
———and J. D. SMITH (1982) "The study of MANOVA effects." Multivariate Behavioral Research 17: 417-432.
ITO, P. K. (1980) "Robustness of ANOVA and MANOVA test procedures," in P. R. Krishnaiah (ed.) Handbook of Statistics, Volume 1: Analysis of Variance. New York: Elsevier North Holland.
———(1969) "On the effect of heteroscedasticity and nonnormality upon some multivariate test procedures," in P. R. Krishnaiah (ed.) Multivariate Analysis, Volume 2. New York: Academic.
HUMMEL, T. J. and J. R. SLIGO (1971) "Empirical comparison of univariate and multivariate analyses of variance procedures." Psychological Bulletin 75: 49-57.
JOHNSON, R. and D. WICHERN (1982) Applied Multivariate Statistical Analysis. Englewood Cliffs, NJ: Prentice-Hall.
JONES, L. V. (1966) "Analysis of variance in its multivariate developments," in R. B. Cattell (ed.) Handbook of Multivariate Experimental Psychology. Chicago: Rand McNally.
JORESKOG, K. G., (1978) "Structural analysis of covariance and correlation matrices." Psychometrika 43: 443-477.
———and A. S. GOLDBERGER (1975) "Estimation of a model with multiple indicators and multiple causes of a single latent variable." Journal of the American Statistical Association 70: 631-639.
JORESKOG, K. G. and D. SORBOM (1983) LISREL VI. Chicago: National Educational Resources.
KAPLAN, R. M. and A. J. LITROWNIK (1717) "Some statistical methods for the assessment of multiple outcome criteria in behavioral research." Behavior Therapy 8: 383-392.
KENNY, D. A. (1979) Correlation and Causality. New York: John Wiley.
KIRK, R. E. (1982) Experimental Design. Belmont, CA: Brooks/Cole.
KNAPP, T. R. (1978) "Canonical correlation analysis: a general parametric significance-testing system." Psychological Bulletin 85: 410-416.
LARRABEE, M. J. (1982) "Reexamination of a plea for multivariate analyses." Journal of Counseling Psychology 29: 180-188.
LARZELERE, R. E. and S. A. MULAIK (1977) "Single-sample tests for many correlations." Psychological Bulletin 84: 557-569.
LEARY, M. R. and E. M. ALTMAIER (1980) "Type I error in counseling research: a plea for multivariate analyses." Journal of Counseling Psychology 27: 611-615.
MARASCUILO, L. A. and J. R. LEVIN (1983) Multivariate Statistics in the Social Sciences: A Researcher's Guide. Belmont, CA: Brooks/Cole.
MARDIA, K. V. (1971) "The effects of nonnormality on some multivariate tests and robustness to nonnormality in the linear model." Biometrika 58: 105-121.
MAXWELL, S. E., R. D. ARVEY, and C. J. CAMP (1981) "Measures of strength of association: a comparative examination." Journal of Applied Psychology 66: 525-534.

McCALL, R. B. and M. E. APPELBAUM (1973) "Bias in the analysis of repeated-measures designs: some alternative approaches." Child Development 44: 401-415.

MENDOZA, J. L., V. H. MARKOS, and R. GONTER (1978) "A new perspective on sequential testing procedures in canonical analysis: a Monte Carlo evaluation." Multivariate Behavioral Research 13: 371-382.

MEREDITH, W. (1964) "Canonical correlation with fallible data." Psychometrika 29: 55-65.

MILLER, R. P. (1966) Simultaneous Statistical Inferences. New York: McGraw-Hill.

MORRISON, D. F. (1976) Multivariate Statistical Methods. New York: McGraw-Hill.

MULAIK, S. A. (1975) "Confirmatory factory analysis," in D. J. Amick and H. J. Walberg (eds.) Introductory Multivariate Analysis for Educational, Psychological, and Social Research. Berkeley, CA: McCutchan.

MULLER, K. E. and B. L. PETERSON (1984) "Power analysis for multivariate linear models: new results and SAS makes it practical," in 1984 SUGI Proceedings. Cary, NC: SAS Institute.

NAMBOODIRI, K. (1984) Matrix Algebra: An Introduction. Beverly Hills, CA: Sage.

O'GRADY, K. E. (1978) "Comments on 'some statistical methods for the assessment of multiple outcome criteria in behavioral research.'" Behavior Therapy 9: 471-473.

OLSON, C. L. (1979) "Practical considerations in choosing a MANOVA test statistic: a rejoinder to Stevens." Psychological Bulletin 86: 1350-1352.

———(1976) "On choosing a test statistic in multivariate analysis of variance." Psychological Bulletin 83: 579-586.

———(1974) "Comparative robustness of six tests in multivariate analysis of variance." Journal of the American Statistical Association 69: 894-908.

OVERALL, J. E. and C. J. KLETT (1972) Applied Multivariate Analysis. New York: McGraw-Hill.

PILLAI, K.C.S. (1960) Statistical Tables for Tests of Multivariate Hypotheses. Manila: University of the Philippines, Statistical Center.

POREBSKI, O. R. (1966a) "On the interrelated nature of the multivariate statistics used in discriminatory analysis." British Journal of Mathematical and Statistical Psychology 19: 197-214.

———(1966b) "Discriminatory and canonical analysis of technical college data." British Journal of Mathematical and Statistical Psychology 19: 215-236.

PRUZEK, R. M. (1971) "Methods and problems in the analysis of multivariate data." Review of Educational Research 41: 163-190.

RAMSEY, P. H. (1982) "Empirical power of procedures for comparing two groups on p variables." Journal of Educational Statistics 7: 139-156.

———(1980) "Choosing the most powerful pairwise multiple comparison procedure in multivariate analysis of variance." Journal of Applied Psychology 65: 317-326.

RAO, C. R. (1951) "An asymptotic expansion of the distribution of Wilks' criterion." Bulletin of the International Statistics Institute 33: 177-180.

RODGER, R. S. (1973) "Confidence intervals for multiple comparisons and the misuse of the Bonferroni inequality." British Journal of Mathematical and Statistical Psychology 26: 58-60.

ROY, J. (1958) "Step-down procedure in multivariate analysis." Annuals of Mathematical Statistics 29: 1177-1187.

————and R. E. BARGMANN (1958) "Test of multiple independence and the associated confidence bounds." Annuals of Mathematical Statistics 29: 491-503.

SERLIN, R. C. (1982) "A multivariate measure of association based on the Pillai-Bartlett procedure." Psychological Bulletin 91: 413-417.

SPECTOR, P. E. (1980) "Redundancy and dimensionality as determinants of data analytic strategies in multivariate analysis of variance." Journal of Applied Psychology 65: 237-239.

————(1977) "What to do with significant multivariate effects in multivariate analyses of variance." Journal of Applied Psychology 62: 158-163.

STEVENS, J. P. (1984) "An easily implemented graphical test for multivariate normality." (unpublished manuscript)

————(1980) "Power of the multivariate analysis of variance tests." Psychological Bulletin 88: 728-737.

————(1979) "Comment on Olson: on choosing a test statistic in multivariate analysis of variance." Psychological Bulletin 86: 355-360.

————(1973) "Step-down analyses and simultaneous confidence intervals in MANOVA." Multivariate Behavioral Research 8: 391-402.

————(1972) "Four methods of analyzing between variation for the K-Group MANOVA problem." Multivariate Behavioral Research 7: 499-522.

STRAHAN, R. I. (1982) "Multivariate analysis and the problem of Type I error." Journal of Counseling Psychology 29: 175-179.

TATSUOKA, M. M. (1977) "Review of Multivariate Statistical Methods in Behavioral Research by R. D. Bock." Applied Psychological Measurement 1: 457-461.

————(1973) "Multivariate analysis in educational research," in F. N. Kerlinger (ed.) Review of Research in Education. Itasca, IL: Peacock.

————(1971) Multivariate Analysis: Techniques for Educational and Psychological Research. New York: John Wiley.

————(1970) Discriminant Analysis: The Study of Group Differences. Champaign, IL: IPAT.

————(1969) "Multivariate analysis." Review of Educational Research 39: 739-743.

THOMPSON, B. (forthcoming) Canonical Correlation. Beverly Hills, CA: Sage.

THORNDIKE, R. M. and D. J. WEISS (1973) "A study of the stability of canonical correlations and canonical components." Educational and Psychological Measurements 33: 123-134.

TIMM, N. H. (1975) Multivariate Analysis: With Applications in Education and Psychology. Belmont, CA: Brooks/Cole.

VAN DE GEER, J. P. (1971) Introduction to Multivariate Analysis for the Social Sciences. San Francisco: Freeman.

WILKINSON, L. (1975) "Response variable hypothesis in the multivariate analysis of variance." Psychological Bulletin 82: 408-412.

YAO, Y. (1965) "An approximate degrees of freedom solution to the multivariate Behrens-Fisher problem." Biometrika 52: 139-147.

JAMES H. BRAY is Associate Professor of Psychology at Texas Woman's University, Houston Center. Dr. Bray earned his B.S., M.A., and Ph.D. degrees from the University of Houston. His doctorate is in clinical psychology, with a minor in research methodology. His research interests include applied statistics, clinical research methodology, and family studies and development. Dr. Bray is the author of several articles appearing in publications such as Review of Educational Research, Journal of Educational Psychology, *and* Journal of Marital and Family Therapy.

SCOTT E. MAXWELL is Associate Professor of Psychology at the University of Notre Dame. He has also taught at the University of Houston, University of North Carolina, and Duke University. He received his undergraduate degree from Duke University and his Ph.D. in quantitative psychology from the University of North Carolina. His research interests include applied statistics and research methodology. Dr. Maxwell is the author of numerous articles appearing in publications such as Review of Educational Research, Annual Review of Psychology, *and* Psychological Bulletin.